BEST GREEN DRINKS EVER

BEST
GREEN
DRINKS
EVER

BOOST YOUR JUICE WITH ANTIOXIDANTS, PROTEIN AND MORE

katrine van wyk

Foreword by Frank Lipman, M.D.

Published by The Countryman Press, P.O. Box 748, Woodstock, VT 05091

Distributed by W. W. Norton & Company, Inc., 500 Fifth Avenue, New York, NY 10110

Printed in the United States

Best Green Drinks Ever

ISBN 978-1-58157-227-8

10 9 8 7 6 5 4 3 2 1

Photo credits: Roald van Wyk: 11, 12, 15, 18, 19, 21, 22, 33, 34, 53, 56, 64, 65, 66, 70, 72, 76, 78, 82, 86, 89, 90, 95, 96, 102, 110, 116, 119, 120, 123, 124, 128, 130, 132, 136, 139, 140, 143, 155, 156, 159, 162, 166, 176, 180, 185, 186, 192; Katrine van Wyk: 29; Patryce Bak: 9, 10, 63, 68-69, 106, 182; Even André Rygg: 16-17; Winnie Abramson, www.healthygreenkitchen.com, 55, 101

Cover photographs: peaches © Yasonya/iStockphoto.com; pouring juice © kazoka/Shutterstock.com; juice in mason jar © Winnie Abramson; cherries © Linda Shutoff/Shutterstock.com; avocado smoothie © mama_mia/Shutterstock.com; chia seeds © stockcam; kale leaf © JKB Stock/Shutterstock.com; lettuce © Hareluya/Shutterstock.com; author © Patryce Bak.

*To my little prince Felix, who grew healthy and strong
inside me during the creation of this book.*

CONTENTS

FOREWORD / 8
PREFACE: My Green Journey / 12

PART ONE: green drink basics

The Why and How of Green Drinks / 19

About Those Greens / 28

Healthy Boosts and Superfoods / 36

Keep in Mind / 54

Smoothie Bases / 60

PART TWO: green drink recipes

Detox / 73

Immunity Green Smoothie
Bittersweet Symphony
Coconut Greens
Pineapple Greens
Grapefruit Greens
Refresh Smoothie
Green Power Bliss
OJ and Greens
Greenest Green
The Green Master

Dandelion Detox
Dandelion Bliss
Fall into Winter Greens
Green Goddess Smoothie
Jicama-Cilantro Slush
Cilantro Fiesta Juice
All Greens Juice
Beet It Juice
Green Monster Juice

Recharge / 107

C Booster
Copacabana
Seeds of Change
Açai Green
Power Breakfast
Purple and Green

Whey to Go!
PB and Jelly
Winter Wonder
Jessica Rabbit Juice
"V8" Garden Juice

Vitality / 129

Peachy Green
Hail to the Kale
Kiwi, Spinach, and Avocado
Apple Pie
Sweet Almond Kale
Green Mojito
Banana Chard
Morning Sun
Frozen Green Lemonade

Mango Madness
Northern Lights
Red and Ready
The Kiwi
The Bee-utiful
Watermelon Medley Juice
Cucumber Cooler Juice
Skin Tonic Juice
Good Greens Juice

Energy / 163

The Green Kiss
Mint Chocolate Chip Shake
Go-Go Goji
Hypnoparadise
Strawberry Fields

Spiritual Gangster
Matcha Shake
Super Brazilian
Cool It Green Juice
Kale Energizer Juice

Digestion / 183

Fiber Blend
Piña Colada
Belly Soother
Blueberry Lassi

Pineapple Express
Juice
Green Juice Light
Fine Fennel Juice

INDEX / 196
ACKNOWLEDGMENTS / 200

FOREWORD

Lose weight! Boost immunity! Improve your love life! If there were a pharmaceutical drug that did all three, there'd be a stampede to the pharmacy, but for now, no such pill exists. My advice? Build your own—not a pill, but a plan, an eating strategy that packs power, nutritional value, and a host of benefits into every bite. *Best Green Drinks Ever* can be your first step to making such a plan.

I practice what I call "good medicine," combining the best of modern contemporary medicine with the best of alternative and complementary medicines. This is where Katrine van Wyk and her delicious recipes come into play. Food is critical in building and sustaining a healthy lifestyle—it's an easy first step, in fact, as we all need to eat.

> Calorie for calorie, leafy greens deliver more nutrients than just about any other food on the planet.

Katrine provides nutritional guidance to patients in my practice as part of my system for nourishing from the inside out. In *Best Green Drinks Ever,* she brings that experience beyond the office and into the real world. Her words of encouragement and advice, the appealing photographs, and the simplicity of her recipes will inspire you to try tossing some greens into your blender.

Smoothies and fresh vegetable juices give you a direct shot of vitamins, minerals, phytonutrients, and enzymes. Juicing will give you a boost of energy like no other, while giving your digestion a break at the same time. Smoothies provide a steady supply of energy, and keep you satisfied with fiber, protein, and the addition of superfood boosts.

Leafy greens are behind the vivid color pop for these drinks, but don't let that scare you off. Fruits, herbs, and other ingredients help make these green drinks easy to add to your diet. And the leafy greens are what make these drinks truly the best.

Calorie for calorie, leafy greens deliver more nutrients than just about any other food on the planet. Loaded with fiber, vitamins, minerals, and phytochemicals, leafy greens stock your body with the artillery needed to fight off potential killers like heart disease and cancer. Simply put: leafys benefit virtually every cell you've got!

Katrine uses lots of my favorite leafy greens in *Best Green Drinks Ever*. Kale, spinach, Swiss chard, mustard, and dandelion greens rock because they're both nutritious and delicious. By juicing them or tossing them into a smoothie, you'll be receiving health-sustaining doses of vitamins A, C, and K, folate, potassium, and calcium. Katrine also provides the option of an easy added boost with greens powder added to your smoothies.

At the Eleven Eleven Wellness Center, we encourage our patients to become proactive in their own health, and partner with them as they journey towards true health and optimal wellness. With her book *Best Green Drinks Ever*, Katrine van Wyk helps guide her readers to good health.

—Frank Lipman, M.D.

A pioneer and internationally recognized expert in the fields of integrative and functional medicine, Dr. Frank Lipman is the founder and director of Eleven Eleven Wellness Center in New York City, where his personal brand of healing has helped thousands of people reclaim their vitality and recover their zest for life.

I came to New York City from Norway eight years ago as a model. I walked the streets and catwalks of this big city, constantly being judged on my size, appearance, skin, hair, and overall "look." Yet I didn't feel all that well on the inside. I was careful about what I ate, to a point of obsession, and exercised way too much. I knew that eating healthy was important—but I was confused about what that really meant. I relied on caffeine and sugar to get me through the long days, and couldn't help but count the calories of everything I ingested. Not so fun!

I was a young girl, but I was not healthy—yet there I was, supposedly a model and image of what was considered ideal. I just did not feel good about all of that. And so, I quit.

I went back to school to finish my undergrad degree in Media Science and finally freed myself from all the judging eyes of the fashion industry. And so a journey began to figure out who I was, what I liked, and what made me feel good. After depleting my body of all the nutrients it needed, it was time to rebuild and restore. Nutrient-dense foods like leafy greens became an important part of my diet, and I finally pinpointed a few food intolerances. At first my new lifestyle made me feel restricted and deprived, but with the help of a health coach I discovered many other healthy foods. It was like a whole new world opened up to me—a delicious world filled with kale, green juices, and colorful smoothies.

Once I removed those damaging foods from my diet and forgot about dieting and restriction, I started feeling better. I gained back my energy, and then some, once I started including more nutrient-dense foods into my life. It turned out that my body had been worn down and depleted after all those years of modeling, traveling, and overworking. I felt incredibly empowered knowing that I could change the way I felt through what I ate. I had gained control of my wellness.

I learned that a calorie is not a calorie and that the quality and wholesomeness of the food I eat matters the most. It is important to eat real foods that contain nutrients instead of just counting calories. A 100-calorie snack of an organic apple is going to nourish you, giving you sustainable energy and nutrients, while the same amount of calories coming from a bag of mini cookies will cause your blood sugar to spike and then come crashing down. I learned that real foods are always superior and that fat is good for me. Now I have a newfound love affair with avocados, coconuts, and real butter. I learned that pleasure, fun, and enjoyment are part of a healthy life and that the setting where we eat and share a meal matters a lot. And I learned that food can be medicine and that the body can heal itself. I found foods that I love and that love me back. And, finally, I learned that I'll always keep learning, exploring, experimenting, and evolving. It's what it's all about!

And so I knew that I wanted to be part of the solution—to share what I had learned and help others feel the best they could. I went back to school again, this time to the Institute for Integrative Nutrition, and got certified as a Holistic Health Coach. I started working with people one-on-one—watching them learn, grow, and feel better. One client managed to stop her diet-soda addiction (she used to drink twelve cans a day!) and lost ten pounds in the process. Another woman discovered that gluten had been one of the big culprits for her declining health, her heartburn, her debilitating headaches. I started doing consulting work and training for juice and smoothie bars. I joined Dr. Frank Lipman's wellness practice, where I keep meeting inspiring people, hearing incredible stories of recovery, and continuing to dig deeper into the holistic health world.

I am a lucky girl who grew up with a mom who cooked and included me and my sister in the kitchen activities. We were allowed to participate and experiment, and my mom never used a recipe. A little bit of this and little bit of that—and voilà!

Cut to twenty years later and I'm back in the kitchen experimenting, this time with all things leafy and green and some fun gadgets to turn solids into liquids. My love for leafy greens—and my blender and juicer—led me to write this book. I truly hope you find it inspiring, fun, and delicious. My goal is to inspire you to have fun in the kitchen and enjoy healthy food simply because it tastes so good. Healthy living should be fun and rewarding, jam-packed with beautiful and nutritious food. I hope you find as much fun and enjoyment in trying these recipes as I had in making them. Here's to you and to no more diets!

All my best wishes for your own healthy journey!

—Katrine van Wyk

PART ONE

GREEN DRINK BASICS

**THE WHY AND HOW
OF GREEN DRINKS** / 19

ABOUT THOSE GREENS / 28

**HEALTHY BOOSTS
AND SUPERFOODS** / 36

KEEP IN MIND / 54

SMOOTHIE BASES / 60

THE WHY AND HOW OF GREEN DRINKS

Why Drink Green Smoothies and Juices?

What are the benefits of drinking your nutrients? Maybe you've even been told to be careful not to drink your calories, or that fruit juices are not healthy at all. Well, there is certainly some truth to that—so what makes fresh smoothies and juices so much better?

Fresh smoothies are packed with nutrients: vitamins, minerals, amino acids, healthy fats, and lots of fiber! Most smoothies and juices you buy at the supermarket have been pasteurized—a process that kills bacteria and prolongs shelf life, but also causes major loss of nutrients and beneficial enzymes.

One common culprit of hunger and cravings is actually dehydration. When the body is dehydrated, we feel tired and sluggish and very often start craving sugar or caffeine to help pick ourselves up. But that just makes us even more dehydrated, and off we go! Smoothies are packed with nourishing, hydrating fruits and vegetables. While it's great to drink pure water, we also need electrolytes in order to absorb the water properly. Many of the smoothies in this book contain coconut water—nature's very own sports drink—as well as bananas and other potassium-rich foods that help prevent muscle cramping and dehydration. In addition we have smoothies with cucumber, watermelon, citrus, and green apple—all foods that are very high in water.

Another culprit for cravings and hunger is nutrient deficiency. Did you know that even though many of us are overweight and struggle to lose weight, we are also undernourished? Too many of the foods we eat are depleted of nutrients or, even worse, actually deplete our bodies of nutrients. Sugar and white flour are high on the list, along with processed, chemical-laden foods that are foreign and damaging to our intestines. When you start eating more nutrient-dense foods, such as fresh smoothies, you'll replenish many of those much-needed nutrients. Fresh fruits and vegetables that have been grown outside in the sunshine harvest the energy of the sun. The more light a fruit or vegetable is able to store, the more nutritious it is. This stored energy finds its way from the food that we eat into our cells. Pretty cool, right?

As you include more of these fresh foods in your life, you'll start feeling yourself have more energy, your mood will improve, and your general satisfaction will increase. And all those cravings? They'll slowly and steadily diminish as your body's nutrient storage fills back up.

JUICING VS. BLENDING: WHAT'S THE DIFFERENCE?

Smoothies are blended drinks made with fresh or frozen fruits and/ or vegetables that get processed together in a blender. A juice, on the other hand, is made by pressing out all the juice from fruits and vegetables using a juicer and then discarding the pulp or fiber left behind.

While green juice is stripped of all fiber and therefore provides a quick shot of energy and vitality to our body, a green smoothie is packed with filling fiber and is therefore a perfect breakfast or snack that will make you feel full and satisfied. I love to drink both and suggest you incorporate some liquid greens in some form into your daily life.

Why Drink Green Smoothies?

Because smoothies have been pre-blended for you, your digestive system doesn't have to work as hard in order to break down the food and get to those nutrients. I doubt you chew your food into the same liquid form as a smoothie! This gives your digestive system a bit of a break to focus on its important processes—including elimination of toxins and nutrient absorption.

Smoothies are one of my go-to choices for breakfast, especially when I'm in a hurry. I can quickly throw some nutritious foods in my blender, switch it on, take two deep breaths, switch it off—and breakfast is served. If you don't have time to sip it slowly at home, pour it into a jar and take it to go. Just don't skip breakfast!

Another great benefit to smoothies is that it's easy to sneak in some super-healthy ingredients that you may not tend to eat enough of—such as leafy greens, seeds, or superfoods. Smoothies are great for kids who don't like to eat their veggies. Throw a handful of spinach into a berry smoothie and they will never even know what hit them.

Why Drink Green Juices?

Fresh fruit and vegetable juices work like an IV nutrient shot. Because we've removed the pulp from these plants and only drink the pure liquid, our bodies absorb the nutrients very quickly without our digestive systems having to do much work. The process of extracting the juice breaks down the plant cell walls and makes it easy for the digestive enzymes in our bodies to act on these different nutrients. One thing to be cautious of when drinking a lot of juices is the sugar content. Exactly because the fiber is removed, the sugar from these fruits and vegetables also gets absorbed quickly and can cause blood sugar to spike. Be cautious about drinking too many fruit-based juices. Instead opt for an 80/20 blend of vegetables and fruits, and use fresh herbs, lemon, lime, and ginger to give your juice a lot of fresh flavor without all the sugar.

And last, but obviously not least, smoothies and juices are totally delicious and fun! Allow your palate, pantry, and mood to decide and have some fun. Look at this as your very own health insurance plan. You are investing in your own health for the long haul! There are plenty of recipes in this book to help you get started, but don't let that limit you. Try out your very own combinations, variations, and creative expressions.

Equipment: What Do I Need to Get Started?

The good news is that you really don't have to spend a lot of money on fancy equipment in order to get started. There are so many different juicers and blenders on the market that you're sure to find one in your price range. If you have a high-power blender you can actually make juices with it by straining the blended drink. Or you can get a great juicer that will turn your kale, apples, celery, and beets into fiberless liquid elixirs.

Blenders

HIGH-POWER BLENDERS

Full disclosure: Vitamix is the blender I used when developing all the recipes in this book and is without a doubt my blender of choice. It is extremely powerful, fast, and easy to use. What makes the Vitamix (and other powerful, high-speed blenders like it) so special is its ability to finely blend hard fruits such as apples, ice, and leafy greens such as kale. I have friends who swear by Blendtec, however. It's a matter of personal preference and the size of your wallet—high-power blenders can range in price from about $200 to over $1,000. You might also look into refurbished blenders sold by the manufacturer. If

HOW TO BUILD A SMOOTHIE

Even though I'm providing you with quite a few recipes in this book, at some point you might want to start exploring and making up your own blends based on what's in season or your fridge! When building a green smoothie there are three main components: the liquid base, the leafy green, and the fruit. Optional ingredients may include some healthy fat, a booster, some fresh herbs, and/or protein powder.

Start by adding your fruit and greens to the blender. Add any powders, fats, or seeds on top and then pour the liquid base over all the ingredients. That way the hardest ingredients to blend are closest to the blender blades, and the liquid gets distributed throughout the other ingredients to help blend everything with ease. You can also try adding the liquid first. With some blenders that works a lot better, so read the instructions that come with your specific blender and try it a few different ways to find out what really works best for your blender.

Blend all the ingredients well before adding any additional water or ice. Always taste your drink before adding any extra sweetener. You may be surprised how much sweet goodness comes out of those fresh foods. A last little tip for all you new green smoothie drinkers—they usually taste even better when they are nice and cold. Feel free to add ice to any recipe—even if it's not mentioned—to make the smoothie ice-cold!

you know you are going to make a lot of green smoothies and enjoy cooking, consider a high-speed blender as a long-term investment. Buying smoothies and juices soon adds up to the cost of one of these blenders. If those aren't an option, less expensive Ninja blenders work very well for the price.

BULLETS

These are super convenient, small, and travel-friendly blenders such as the NutriBullet and Magic Bullet. They are usually quite powerful blenders, despite their size, and perfect for making a single serving. If you have a very small kitchen, live in a dorm, or travel a lot and still want to have your green drinks, bullet blenders are perfect. They are usually much less expensive than the other options.

KITCHEN BLENDERS

There are lots of options for good kitchen blenders in all price ranges, colors, sizes, and powers. I personally like to avoid plastic as much as possible, so I look for a blender that comes with a glass container. If you already have a blender you're happy with, there's no need to toss it. If it ain't broke . . . Know that because standard kitchen blenders are less powerful, smoothies can come out a little thicker. You can always add more liquid to your smoothies if you're using a regular blender. For the very "green" drinks, a more powerful blender is preferable, as it does a better job at finely chopping up tough greens such as kale.

Juicers

CENTRIFUGAL JUICER

This is a great beginning juicer. It's easy to use and clean and quite affordable, with some models as low as $99. It has a fast-spinning blade that spins the produce against a mesh filter to separate juice from pulp by utilizing centrifugal force. One concern with this method is that the centrifugal spinning generates heat. The heat destroys some of the enzymes, as well as oxidizing and destroying some of the nutrients in the fruits and vegetables you are juicing. So, juice from a centrifugal juicer is less nutritious than juice made in a cold-press juicer. Make sure to drink your juice right away because the juice oxidizes and loses a lot of its nutritional power quickly. If you plan to try juicing but don't expect to make gallons of juice every day, a centrifugal juicer is a great option.

SLOW OR COLD-PRESS JUICER

These are the Rolls-Royce of juicing. Not only do they have a higher price point—closer to $300 to start—they also extract more nutrients and juice out of your produce without adding any heat, which allows the juice to stay fresh longer. While the centrifugal process actually creates heat that can damage the enzymes and nutrients of the fresh fruits and vegetables, a slow juicer uses a "mortar and pestle" extraction technique that doesn't create any heat—hence the name, cold-pressed. I personally have a Hurom juicer and love it. These juicers are great if you're looking to get serious about your juicing or if you'd like your juice to stay fresh for a little longer. As an added bonus, these juicers can also make baby food and nut milk.

Other Handy Equipment to Have

SALAD SPINNER

I love using a salad spinner for washing all my leafy greens and herbs. Soak the leaves in water in the spinner, drain it, and rinse a few times before spinning all the leaves dry. You can also use the spinner to store your now-clean greens in the fridge. It keeps them fresh for days!

NUT-MILK BAG

You certainly don't need one of these, but it does come in handy, especially if you like making your own nut milks or want to make juices using your blender. A nut-milk bag is simply a fine mesh cloth or nylon bag with a string for closing it at the top. Just pour your blended liquid into the bag, let it strain off, and use some squeezing muscle power to "milk" the bag of all its liquids. The pulp remains inside the bag, while you're left with pure liquid goodness! You could also use a sock or folded cheesecloth for the same purpose.

GLASS JARS

Glass jars or jugs such as Mason or Ball jars are great for drinking and transporting your green drinks! Because they have a nice wide opening, they are easy to fill, drink from, and clean.

STRAWS

Sure, you do not need to drink your green drinks with a straw, but it can be helpful in order to avoid a green mustache. I like glass or stainless-steel straws that I can wash in the dishwasher and use over and over again. Paper straws are also great, and biodegradable.

HOW TO BUILD A JUICE

When making a green juice, start off with a vegetable high in water such as cucumber or celery. If you want a milder, smoother-tasting juice, go with cucumber, and if you want a more pungent juice, celery is the way to go. Then pick your leafy greens. You can use just one or a combination of many. While romaine has a mild flavor, the flavor of Swiss chard or kale is stronger. Then add one or two fruits of your choice; green apple, pear, and pineapple are my favorites. Last add your flavor bonuses: lime, lemon, fresh herbs, or ginger.

Before making a juice, wash all ingredients thoroughly and do all the necessary chopping and peeling (you may only need to peel the lemon and lime). Depending on your juicer you might be able to keep every-thing in large chunks and the kale leaves whole, or you might have to cut it all up quite well.

Switch the juicer on before starting to feed it. Alternate between leafy greens, fruit, herbs, and your base (cucumber or celery). The leafy greens tend to be harder work for the juicer, and a little more liquid from the fruit or celery helps it all along. I also find that when I alter-nate like this I tend to get less foam on my juice.

ABOUT THOSE GREENS

I tell all my clients to eat more leafy greens.
A lot of us forget about this large group of
delicious vegetables and get stuck in a rut
with just baby carrots and tomato sauce as our
main vegetable sources. Focus especially on
the dark, leafy greens like kale, Swiss chard,
dandelion (who knew?), spinach, and mustard
greens. These dark and leafy greens are high in
micronutrients such as magnesium, calcium,
folate, and vitamins A, C, and K, and if you're
blending, not juicing, fiber.

Greens are especially beneficial in the
spring as they aid in the body's natural detox
process—out with the old, in with the new!

Benefits of eating more greens include:

- Aiding the body's natural detox process
- Glowing skin
- Satisfaction and reduced cravings
- Increased energy
- Alkalizing and cleansing the body
- Uplifting and positive energy
- Boosting cardiovascular health
- Fighting free radicals with high levels of antioxidants
- Protection against disease
- Improving bone health

LEAFY GREENS

romaine

Surprisingly romaine lettuce contains quite a bit of protein, about 7 grams per head, and it's a complete protein with all eight essential amino acids that our bodies can't make on their own. It also contains plenty of vitamins A, C, and B and some healthy omega-3 fatty acids. It's also worth mentioning that if you need to limit your intake of oxalic acid (due to calcium oxalate kidney stones, for example), romaine is a good choice.

spinach

Spinach is Popeye's fuel of choice for good reason. In addition to being high in the nutrients mentioned above, spinach contains high levels of betaine, which regulates proper homocysteine levels and supports the liver. It is also a good source of zinc and iron.

kale

Kale has been celebrated as quite the superfood recently and for good reason! This cruciferous family member contains many cancer-fighting nutrients. The high level of vitamin A is great for our lungs and skin, while vitamin C boosts our immune system and K protects our bones. Kale also contains plenty of glucosinolate and cysteine sulfoxide, which can help switch on the liver's detoxifying enzymes. Pretty cool stuff!

swiss chard

This relative of the beet and spinach is high in vitamin K, a nutrient many of us just don't get enough of. Vitamin K plays an important role in protecting our bones, reduces the risk of cardiovascular disease and stroke, and helps cool down inflammation. Swiss chard often has a bright pink or yellow stem, which can add a pretty color to your plate or juice.

cucumber

Although not a leafy green vegetable, cucumbers are still green and a great addition to green juices and drinks. Cucumber is known for its hydrating and cooling benefits. And cucumber does more than just hydrate. Its high level of silica (a mineral) does wonders for our connective tissue—especially our skin, both when ingested and when used topically.

celery

Celery is easily available and a very affordable vegetable, making it a great base for green juices. It has wonderful anti-inflammatory properties and is high in phytonutrients. Celery can also help aid digestion and if eaten (not juiced) contains lots of fiber to help keep our bowels regular.

Benefits of Seasonal Fruits and Vegetables

- **FLAVOR:** Produce that has been allowed to ripen fully in the sun tastes amazing! Freshly picked produce has optimal flavor—crispy, fragrant, juicy, and colorful. A summer heirloom tomato makes all other tomatoes seem inferior. You can eat it like an apple: raw, warm from the sun, and straight from the vine.

- **NUTRITION:** Plants get their nourishment from the sun and soil. Seasonally fresh produce is picked when it's ripe and fully developed. The plant has had more sun exposure, which means it will have higher levels of antioxidants. Studies have also found that the level of iodine and beta-carotene in milk is higher in the summer than in the winter months—ice cream, anyone?

- **ECONOMY:** It's simply supply and demand. When there's an abundance of a product, such as watermelons in the summer, the prices go down. Seasonal food is much cheaper to produce for the farmers, who would rather sell their products for a lower price than not at all. Cash in on the seasonal bounty.

- **ENVIRONMENT:** Seasonal produce can grow without too much added human assistance such as pesticides and genetic modification. We know how the toxic compounds in pesticides and insecticides can contaminate the water and soil and also our health. Seasonal food is more likely to be locally produced as well, which reduces the load on our environment due to transport, or "food mileage."

- **COMMUNITY:** Getting to know where your food is coming from, who is growing your food, and how they do it also makes you feel more connected to that whole process. Community-supported agriculture farms (CSAs) and farmers' markets create communities around food that encourage us all to share our knowledge, ask questions, and engage in our own local environment. Together we are more powerful and that's when big change can happen.

- **HOME COOKING:** Eating seasonally also encourages you to cook more—and there really is nothing better you could do for your health. When you start to take back control of what you put into your body—which oil you choose to cook with, how much sugar you add to your food, etc.—you are consciously making better choices for yourself. Cooking is also a great activity to do with your whole family and your friends. What better way to show your love than with a home-cooked meal?

- **CREATIVITY AND VARIETY:** Whether you shop at the market or you're part of a CSA, eating seasonally keeps challenging your creativity to come up with new, fun, and delicious dishes based on what you find. Maybe you choose to search for a recipe online, look through some cookbooks, or go to sites like Pinterest (I'm obsessed with it, and you can find me and follow my boards if you're into that kind of thing!) to find new inspiration and ideas about what to do with all that kale. Variety is also healthy for our bodies; by changing your menu according to what's available seasonally you are less likely to develop food intolerances.

- **SUPPORT OF YOUR SEASONAL NEEDS:** The natural cycle of produce is perfectly designed to support our health. Apples grow in the fall and they are the perfect transition food, helping the body get rid of excess heat and cool down before winter. In the spring the abundance of leafy greens helps us alkalize, detox, and lose some extra pounds after a long winter of heavier foods. In the summer we need to cool down and stay hydrated by eating more juicy fruits, antioxidant-rich berries, and hydrating cucumber and watermelon, to name just a few. Building a lifestyle around seasonal food facilitates the body's natural healing process.

- **ORGANIC AND FREE OF PESTICIDES:** Food grown outside of its season or natural environment needs a lot more human assistance in the form of pesticides, waxes, chemicals, and preservatives to grow and look appealing to us as consumers. So, by instead opting for local and seasonal food, you are also more likely to get a cleaner product! Many small family farms cannot afford to go through the organic certification process, but still follow very natural and sustainable growing practices. So, when shopping at the farmers' market, you don't have to be as careful about finding the organic-labeled produce as you are when shopping at the supermarket.

- **HARMONY:** Living in tune with nature's rhythm makes us more aware and appreciative of the beauty around us. We can live in balance with our surroundings instead of constantly butting up against and living in conflict with nature. Embracing the natural rhythm of things also helps simplify our lives. The options are limited and we can trust that our food is nourishing and good for us!

GREENS AND THYROID ISSUES

Got thyroid issues? A word of caution: Raw greens from the brassica family (cabbage, spinach, kale, collards, etc.) contain glucosinolates, which can inhibit iodine uptake and act as a goitrogen (goitrogens are substances that can suppress thyroid function). For people with thyroid issues, drinking and eating too much of these vegetables in their raw state can  further agitate their condition. Instead, rotate your greens to prevent buildup of oxalic acid, which can affect the thyroid. Also, know that saturated fat and avocado are foods that actually help stimulate thyroid function, so don't skimp on the fats!

If you have thyroid issues, I suggest using romaine lettuce as your leafy green instead of kale or spinach most of the time. Some raw kale or spinach from time to time is absolutely fine, but if you get on the smoothie bandwagon and start making a green drink every day (you go!), it's worth mixing up your greens!

In general, remember that variety is the spice of life! Not only does it help keep your taste buds happy, choosing different fruits and vegetables ensures a variety of nutrients too.

What to Buy Organic

- When buying produce and ingredients for your juice and smoothies, always choose the best quality possible. USDA certified organic means that the food has not been treated with synthetic pesticides or fertilizers. No genetic engineering, antibiotics, or hormones can be used. More and more research is coming out about how dangerous some of the most commonly used pesticides can be for us humans. But not only that, they are harmful for our planet too. Pesticides and fertilizers pollute drinking water and upset the natural balance of the surrounding ecosystem. GMO (genetically modified organism) foods have been identified as possible causes of the increase in food sensitivities and digestive issues. Thankfully most of the GMO crops make their way into processed and packaged foods and not our fresh fruit and vegetables. The only exceptions are some zucchini, sweet corn, and Hawaiian papaya.

- Organic fruits and vegetables are often grown in a soil that is much less depleted of minerals, which means the vegetables end up with a higher nutrient content, too!

- Because organic farming practices can be a little more labor-intensive and expensive for the farmer, organically grown fruits and vegetables tend to cost a little bit more money for consumers. I firmly believe that buying good quality, healthy food is an investment in long-term health and well-being—it's the best health insurance money can buy!

- However, sometimes we simply cannot find or afford to buy everything organic. I know I can't! So, it's good to know which fruits and vegetables we absolutely should buy organic, and which are less important. The Environmental Working Group (ewg.org) tests fruits and vegetables for their pesticide content and lists the most and least contaminated foods on their website. The list is updated from time to time, but here's what it revealed as I was writing this book.

THE DIRTY DOZEN

These fruits and vegetables
you should always buy organic:

1. Apples
2. Celery
3. Cherry tomatoes
4. Cucumbers
5. Grapes
6. Hot peppers
7. Nectarines
8. Peaches
9. Potatoes
10. Spinach
11. Strawberries
12. Sweet bell peppers

THE CLEAN FIFTEEN

These you don't have to buy organic:

1. Asparagus
2. Avocados
3. Cabbage
4. Cantaloupe
5. Eggplant
6. Grapefruit
7. Kiwi
8. Mangos
9. Mushrooms
10. Onions
11. Papaya
12. Pineapple
13. Sweet corn
14. Sweet peas
15. Sweet potatoes

Lists from ewg.org, EWG's Shopper's Guide to Pesticides

- As a general rule, buy organic if you are going to eat (or juice) the peel of the fruit or vegetable. You can be more lenient with fruits and vegetables with thick skin that you will peel away. Fruits with thin or porous skin, such as berries, peaches, and grapes, as well as leafy greens, are the ones it is most important to buy organic.

- Remember, organic frozen fruits and vegetables are a great option. Whenever I shop I always make sure to grab a bag of organic blueberries and another fruit I'm in the mood for so that I always have something healthy and delicious ready in the freezer.

HEALTHY BOOSTS AND SUPERFOODS

Good Protein Sources

Protein is often referred to as the body's building blocks. It supplies amino acids that are absolutely necessary for healing and restoring the body. It also helps build muscles. Without adequate protein in our diets we can start feeling weak and low in energy. The good news is that protein can be found in many foods, not just animal meat, eggs, and dairy, but also nuts, seeds, whole grains, and leafy greens. So, no matter what your dietary preference might be, there are some good protein sources out there for you.

I like adding some extra protein to my smoothies when I have them instead of a meal or after a workout. That way I know I'm giving my body all the different nutrients it needs to restore and recover, and it also helps me feel satisfied and full for longer.

There are many different ways to add protein to your smoothies. The easiest way is simply to add a good protein powder. But you can also boost your smoothie with protein-rich foods like whole-milk dairy, eggs, or seeds.

In the chart on page 40, I give you some options. Pick a few that call out to you and try them out in your own smoothies!

A Few Words about Dairy:

- Dairy is certainly a hot topic in the health-food world, and there are a lot of heated opinions out there. I personally believe that everyone is different, and each individual has to find out what works for his or her body. Some people find that they can't tolerate cow's milk well, but that goat or sheep milk products work fine. Others do well eating all kinds of dairy while some prefer sticking to fermented dairy products like yogurt and kefir. Whatever you choose, make a conscious choice and go for organic grass-fed/pastured dairy products. Also, always buy full-fat dairy products. That's right! The fat in dairy is saturated, but it's still good for you. We need the fat to absorb the nutrients that are in the dairy. Also, keep in mind that low-fat or nonfat dairy products are even more processed and are often sweetened to compensate for the lack of delicious-tasting fat.

- If you are lucky enough to live near a farm or a farmers' market where you can get raw dairy, that's even better. Raw dairy has not been pasteurized, and therefore all the enzymes are still intact, including lactase—the enzyme needed to digest (you guessed it!) lactose.

Good Sources of Healthy Fats

The low-fat diet days are long gone. We know better now—our bodies need fat in order to function. Fat is the brain's preferred fuel and does absolute wonders for our skin. Fat also makes our food taste more delicious and helps us feel satisfied and full for longer. Fat is crucial for the absorption of certain vitamins known as fat-soluble vitamins. Studies have even shown that the nutrients in fruits and vegetables are better absorbed by the body when combined with some fat—think salad with full-fat dressing or broccoli with a dollop of butter. By adding healthy fats to our drinks we improve nutrient absorption and satiety, help curb cravings, and aid our body in keeping our blood sugar levels stable. However, not all fats and oils are created equal. And no one needs huge amounts of it—a little goes a long way. Think of a quarter of an avocado as a serving, or 1 tablespoon of nut butter or coconut oil as a good healthy dose for most of us. On the chart on page 42, I've listed the fats I like and use in my drinks.

Good Sources of Fiber

You may have heard about how important fiber is for keeping your digestion regular, but did you know that fiber-rich plants are prebiotics? That means they are food for the healthy bacteria in our gut, helping our flora stay healthy and in balance. Fiber is also important for detoxification and successfully removing toxins from our bodies.

Fiber helps slow down the absorption of sugar into our bloodstream and in that way can decrease drastic spikes in blood sugar. When we have blood sugar levels that take us on a roller-coaster ride all day, from soaring high to crashing hard, we can experience mood swings, fluctuating energy levels, and cravings.

Most vegetables, fruits, nuts, seeds, and whole grains contain good amounts of fiber. And for an added boost to your drinks, I've listed good sources of fiber that you can add to your drinks on page 44.

Superfoods

"Superfoods" is a term that refers to foods that are particularly nutrient dense. We can reap great benefits by adding just small amounts of these foods to our diet. Most of them are loaded with free radical–fighting antioxidants believed to protect our body's cells from damage, premature aging, and even cancer. You'll find many of these superfoods already added to recipes throughout the book, but feel free to add them to whichever drink you want to gain some extra superpowers. Check out the chart on page 46–50 for more details.

GOOD PROTEIN
SOURCES

pea protein

Pea protein powders are derived from peas and are completely vegan and hypoallergenic. They're a great choice for anyone who has allergies or follows a vegan diet. The powder is usually easily digestible by the body and is therefore great for using while doing a detox.

brown rice protein

Isolating the protein from the whole rice grain creates brown rice protein powder. It is generally well absorbed by the body and, as with pea protein, is vegan.

hemp protein

Hemp protein powder is made from ground-up hemp seeds. Although not as high in protein as some of the other options, it's a great choice for a real purist as it is usually the least processed of protein powders. As an added bonus, it also contains plenty of fiber and some healthy fats.

vegan protein blends

There are many vegan protein powder brands on the market now, and many of them contain a blend of all of the above proteins: pea, rice, and hemp. Some also have added vitamins, minerals, fiber, and greens powder. Make sure to read the labels carefully and look out for blends with a lot of added sugar or fructose. You don't need that when you're going to add it to a nice, fruity smoothie!

whey protein

Whey is a protein found in milk. It is especially beneficial for those looking to build some muscle or who are healing from injury. Whey protein has the correct density to provide support for human muscles and provides a broad range of amino acids that the body can use in healing itself. Look for the whey isolate powders, which are the purest, most expensive, and best absorbed. And if the whey is derived from grass-fed cows, that's even better. Even if you are lactose intolerant you should be fine digesting whey, but try it out and see how you feel.

nuts and seeds

Nuts and seeds are great natural sources of protein, too! Some almond milk, a spoonful of nut butter, or even a handful of your favorite nuts can add a nice protein boost to your drinks.

Proteins to Avoid:

- Avoid all protein powders and blends that contain soy or soy protein isolate. Soy proteins are highly processed and far removed from any natural products. Soy is also fairly hard to digest unless it has been fermented (such as in tempeh and miso). Much of the soy found on the market today is derived from GMO crops, which are genetically altered and foreign to our bodies. Another thing to keep in mind about soy is that it contains phytoestrogen that can mimic estrogen in the body. It also contains goitrogens that can cause thyroid imbalances. For all these reasons you won't find soy milk or proteins in any of the recipes in this book, nor in my fridge at home.

- Also, I recommend that you stay away from any powders with high levels of fructose or endless ingredient lists full of unpronounceable words. A general rule of thumb is to keep all the ingredients for your drinks as close to nature as possible.

GOOD SOURCES OF
HEALTHY FATS

coconut oil

Coconut oil is a great source of medium-chain fatty acids (MCFAs), which get turned directly into energy in the body rather than being stored as fat. It is also easy to digest and is known to increase metabolism, so it can aid with weight loss.

Coconut oil is also high in lauric acid, which supports a healthy immune system due to its very powerful antibacterial, antifungal, and antiviral properties. Besides in coconut oil, lauric acid is only found in breast milk. Coconut oil also helps repair and protect your skin from within.

avocado

Avocado is a great source of healthy fat. The fatty acid called oleic acid found in avocados has been shown to lower bad cholesterol. Together with the high level of fat-soluble vitamin E, which can help reduce blood clots, avocados are great food for your heart! Vitamin E is also an antioxidant that helps protect your skin cells from damage. All the good fats in avocado also moisturize the skin from within—or you can mash it up and make a face mask with it. It's all good!

chia seeds

These tiny seeds look a lot like poppy seeds, but pack way more of a nutritional punch. You see, this is the richest plant source of those essential omega-3 fatty acids! We need omega-3s for proper brain and nerve function, yet most of us just don't get enough. Chia seeds are also packed with minerals and contain a lot of fiber, helping to keep you regular. They also have another very cool added benefit—they swell up to five times their size when added to liquid, so they can help you feel full faster and for longer.

flax seeds

Flax seeds are another good source of both omega-3 fats and fiber. Just like avocados, flax seeds contain plenty of vitamin E, making them a great choice for your skin. Flax seeds are readily available almost anywhere these days, and very affordable, too! I recommend grinding the flax seeds to make the fats and nutrients more available to your body. However, if you have a powerful blender, it will do that work for you while it's blending your smoothie. Easy!

hemp seeds

Hemp seeds are a good source of both protein and fat! They contain all essential amino acids and the essential omega-3 fatty acids, which does wonders for both the heart and skin. Hemp seeds contain the minerals magnesium, zinc, iron, and phosphorus as well as a fat called GLA, believed to balance hormones. By blending hemp seeds and water together you can make a simple milk, too.

GOOD SOURCES OF
FIBER

greens

Every single smoothie in this book contains greens in some form, so you'll always get some fiber from them. They also provide you with a bunch of minerals and antioxidants! It's a win-win.

flax seeds

As discussed on page 42, you can buy whole or ground flax seeds, and they are an easy and tasteless addition to any shake. Flax also contains omega-3 fatty acids, something that's hard to find in high doses in plant foods.

chia seeds

As discussed on page 42, chia seeds contain more omega-3 fatty acids than any other food in the plant world. By adding chia seeds to your drink you get both a healthy dose of essential fatty acids and lots of fiber.

psyllium husk

Another powerful seed, psyllium husk is a seed from the plant *Plantago ovata* from India. When soaked in liquid it turns into a solid gel-like consistency. It's often described as having the ability to sweep your intestine clean. This is a really potent fiber with strong cleansing benefits, so make sure to start with a low dose and drink lots of water. (I would only recommend using psyllium husks over short periods of time. Save it for when you do a detox or really need some added fiber after a few weeks of eating poorly.)

fiber powders

Fiber powders are usually made up of a mix of plant-based sources of fiber and many contain both psyllium husk and flax meal (ground flax seeds). Some also contain probiotics and other nutrients that support your digestion. These powders can be a convenient way to get a concentrated dose of fiber in one product, for those times when you really need it, but it's certainly not a necessary addition if you eat lots vegetables and drink your green smoothies!

nut butters

In addition to being a good source of protein and healthy fats, nuts are a good source of fiber. Nut butters are great to add to smoothies because they blend up easily and make the drink richer, creamier, and more filling.

SUPERFOODS

probiotics

- Improve digestion
- Aid in proper nutrient absorption
- Boost the immune system
- Helps with overall well-being

The word *probiotic* literally means "for life," and it refers to good bacteria that populate our gut. Without taking care of our gut flora, we can eat well and still not feel great. So trust your gut, and nourish it with lots of healthy bacteria!

Probiotics can be found in lactofermented foods and beverages such as sauerkraut, kimchi, and kefir. You can try adding some goat kefir or coconut-water kefir to your smoothies for an extra boost. The probiotic drinks tend to have a refreshing, sour taste, so keep that in mind when adding them to your smoothies. You can also get probiotic supplements in the form of powders and capsules. Probiotic supplements are tasteless, so you can easily add them to any smoothie you're making without changing the taste at all.

bee pollen

- High in protein
- Energy booster
- Helps lower cholesterol
- Nutritional powerhouse full of antioxidants and vitamins

These bright yellow and golden pearls are a nutrient powerhouse and contain virtually all the nutrients you need to live. Bee pollen is rich in folate, amino acids, vitamins B, C, D, and E, and many more.

Bee pollen is believed to be the fountain of youth and has been used as a folk remedy for both PMS and enlarged prostate. Today it is most commonly used as an energy booster. Bee pollen can also help fight seasonal pollen allergies!

spirulina

- Great detoxifier
- Good brain food
- Energy booster

Spirulina is a micro-algae rich in nutrients, omega-3s, vitamin B, iron, and magnesium. It also contains astaxanthin, a carotenoid that has been shown to protect our skin and eyes against UV radiation. Spirulina can help encourage and support the growth of a healthy bacterial flora in our gut, helping boost our immune system.

Spirulina does have a slightly green and fishy taste, so start with a small dose and see how it makes you feel. Try adding it to smoothies with banana, coconut water, and other greens to mask the flavor. You can slowly increase the dosage up to 2 tablespoons per serving.

SUPERFOODS

maca

- Provides an energy boost
- Increases stamina and endurance
- Balances hormones, enhances fertility, raises libido
- Aids in memory retention

Maca is a root from the Andes celebrated for centuries for its powerful benefits. You can find maca in capsule form or as a powder that is easy to add to smoothies. Maca has a nice flavor similar to butterscotch and works well in combination with other superfoods like cinnamon and cacao.

açai

- Loaded with antioxidants
- Protection from free-radical damage
- Contains essential healthy fatty acids

This South American berry with a deep, rich purple color is loaded with beneficial antioxidants. In its pure form it is low in sugar too. You can find it in frozen or freeze-dried form and both are easy and absolutely delicious in smoothies.

cacao

- Loaded with antioxidants
- Helps lower blood pressure
- Gives an energy boost
- Can improve your mood!

Cacao is said to be the food with the highest amount of antioxidants. In raw form, cacao powder and cacao nibs contain more than 1,500 beneficial compounds! The flavonoids found in cacao help relax the walls of our cells and blood vessels. This is good news for anyone with high blood pressure. Cacao also contains plenty of the muscle-relaxing mineral magnesium, known to help improve sleep and relieve constipation. And if you feel pleasure and your mood improving when eating chocolate, you can thank the two compounds anandamide and phenylethylamine. Cacao can also help give you a bit of an energy boost. It contains a stimulant called theobromine, which is similar to caffeine but doesn't cause the same "crashed" feeling shortly after consuming it.

SUPERFOODS

goji berries

- Helps eyesight
- Improves sexual function and fertility
- Boosts immune function
- Promotes longevity

This bright little red berry has been used in Chinese medicine for centuries and grows in China and Tibet.

Goji berries are on top of the ORAC (oxygen radical absorbance capacity) list, which measures the free radical–destroying potential of a particular food. They are also a complete protein, containing all the essential amino acids that we need.

ginger

- Powerful anti-inflammatory
- Improves digestion
- Relieves nausea

Ginger is one of the most powerful anti-inflammatory foods out there. Its potent and spicy oils can actually interrupt some of the chemical reactions that happen in our bodies when inflammation is triggered. Its nice spicy kick helps heat the body and is a great addition to juices and smoothies in the colder winter months.

cinnamon

- Reduces chronic inflammation
- Detoxifies the body
- Helps control glucose levels
- Relieves indigestion

Cinnamon is high in manganese, iron, calcium, and fiber, and it adds a wonderful warming flavor to many foods. It helps prevent the growth of bacteria, and is anti-fungal and anti-parasitic as well. It has also been found to reduce the negative effects of a high-fat meal.

Adding Sweetness

Many of the recipes in this book don't contain any additional sweetener aside from the natural sweetness of the fruits and vegetables. However, if you prefer sweeter-tasting drinks, or are still new to the whole green drink concept, you can always add some sweetener. Here are a few good options:

- **DATES:** Dates are great for sweetening smoothies! They are rich in antioxidants, iron, minerals, and tannins, too, so you get a lot of added nutrients with all that sweetness.

- **STEVIA:** Stevia is actually a green leaf (part of the chrysanthemum family) found in South America, and it's reassuring to know that it's been used for centuries! Stevia is not a sugar and it's believed that it does not feed yeast (or candida) or raise the blood sugar.

- **RAW HONEY:** Honey is an ancient food and energy source that has antibacterial and antiviral properties and actually supports our immune system. It even contains antioxidants and can help reduce inflammation.

- **MAPLE SYRUP:** Maple syrup is another natural alternative to sugar, loaded with vitamins and minerals. I love the taste and it works well in creamy smoothies with almond milk. Make sure you get the real deal and not the diluted, processed stuff.

- **COCONUT SYRUP:** Sweetener derived from coconut contains plenty of nutrients and is rich in enzymes, which can help slow down the absorption of sugar into the bloodstream. Coconut sweeteners (you can find nectar and sugar versions) are produced from the sweet juices of coconut palm sugar blossoms and have long been a staple in Southeast Asia.

Beware of Agave!

- I can't mention sweeteners without adding a few words about agave. Although this has been touted as a health food in the last few years, it turns out it's everything but. Most of the agave "nectar" found on the market is actually a highly refined sweetener made from the starchy root of the agave plant, in a process very similar to making high-fructose corn syrup from cornstarch. Agave nectar also contains more fructose than high-fructose corn syrup, and we know that high-fructose sweeteners can make us crave and eat more. So stay clear and choose one of the more natural sweeteners listed above.

KEEP IN MIND

Tips and Tricks for Easy and Speedy Green Drinking

I have picked up some useful tricks over the years and love fine-tuning my smoothie and juice making so that it becomes as easy, doable, and fun as possible.

What's That You Say? You Just Don't Have the Time?

Challenge number one for most of us is time. We always feel stretched for time, running from one thing to the next and just feeling that there simply aren't enough hours in the day. But what if you prioritized a little differently? Or what if you chose to put your own health first, knowing that in the long run, it will pay off? Or what if you planned things a little more ahead of time? Whatever it is that will make you find the time to eat more fresh, whole foods and drink some green drinks, write it down and start today. Make a commitment and prioritize yourself: You can do pretty much anything you put your mind and effort into. On the next page, you'll find some tricks I use to help me put my health first.

Creating a Healthy Habit

- Eating healthy and feeling good go hand in hand. By creating small, healthy habits you also create an overall lifestyle that supports who you are, what you most desire, and what is important to you. It doesn't have to feel like a struggle or a fight. It should feel right, intuitive almost, and certainly doable, easy, and fun. The key is time and a step-by-step approach. You don't have to start by making green juices and smoothies every single day, if you've never made them at all before. Even having a green drink once a week will be a huge step in the right direction. Once you notice how great you feel after drinking one of them, chances are you'll want to do it again. You don't have to force it, punish yourself, or feel guilty. Those emotions are just a waste of time and energy!

Time Savers

- **MAKE A GROCERY LIST:** Be prepared. Write down what you need for making some green drinks during the week ahead. Bring your list to the store and get your stuff! Nothing more, nothing less.

- **MAKE A BIGGER BATCH:** Green smoothies will last fine in the fridge for a couple of days. If you're making a smoothie, double or triple up the serving. Pour yourself a nice big glass and store the rest in the blender or in a glass jug in your fridge for an afternoon snack or tomorrow's breakfast. It will last at least a day. Just stir it up and serve! If you want to store a freshly made juice or a smoothie for a longer period of time, freezing it is the way to go. If you have it handy, add some vitamin C powder to your drink to help preserve the nutrients better. Use ice-cube trays or even freezer bags. (Avoid storing drinks with protein powders or chia seeds, which will usually thicken up too much over time. Instead, blend all the other ingredients and then just stir in your chia seeds or protein powder right before drinking.)

- **PREP AHEAD:** Wash all your greens at once and store them in the salad spinner or another airtight container in your fridge. Wash all your green apples, celery, and cucumber together ahead of time too so that they're ready to go. Same goes for fruits like melon, pineapple, or papaya—peel, cut into cubes, and store in your fridge for easy snacking and smoothie making. Fresh herbs are also easy to clean in a salad spinner. Store unused herbs wrapped in a damp paper towel in an airtight container in your fridge.

- **SHARE THE RESPONSIBILITIES:** Does your partner, roommate, spouse, or child also like green drinks? Take turns making them. Maybe you each make drinks every other day, or get the family together for a massive cook-off every Sunday, prepping vegetables and cooking some dishes for the week.

- **IN A PINCH, MAKE A SMOOTHIE:** There is no denying it—making a juice takes a bit longer, mainly because you have to clean your juicer straight away. So, when in a hurry, throw your favorite foods in the blender, mix it up, pour it into a glass jar, rinse the blender, and run out the door with drink in hand.

- **WITHIN REACH:** When you're getting into the swing of things and find yourself making a green smoothie every morning, rearrange your kitchen so that all your go-to ingredients, boosters, and protein powders are right within reach.

Storage

- **GLASS BOTTLES OR JARS:** Always serve your drinks in glass instead of plastic. The acid from fruits, lemons, and limes releases the toxins from plastic into the drink. Yuck!

- **GLASSWARE:** Get yourself some nice glass storage containers. They are great for storing all kinds of leftovers, not just drinks! Mason jars are so charming, and I always wash and reuse pickle, jam, or tomato jars.

- **MINI COOLER BAG:** If you want to bring your green drinks to work (a great idea) but have a bit of a commute, get yourself a mini cooler bag. The juices and smoothies stay fresh and cool all the way to the office and you'll have an afternoon snack sure to beat any 3 p.m. snack attack. Vending machines be gone!

- **LEMON AND LIME:** Lemon and lime juice contains citric acid, a natural preservative that helps maintain the nutrients and freshness of your drinks. If you plan to save your drink for later, make sure it has some citric acid from one of these fruits.

Money-Saving Tips

- **FROZEN:** Frozen berries, fruits, and vegetables are a good, nutritious alternative to fresh. In fact, testing shows that they contain nearly the exact same amount of vitamins and minerals as fresh produce. Often organic frozen berries cost a lot less than fresh ones and are convenient to keep on hand. They keep a lot longer, and you may even discover how frozen spinach blends almost tastelessly into a smoothie.

- **SEASONAL:** Food that's in season is often in abundance and so the prices go down. Choose foods that are from your local area and in season. Chances are you're getting a good deal!

- **FARMERS' MARKET:** The farmers' market is a great place to shop for what's local and in season. The produce also tends to cost less because the middleman is removed. You are buying straight from the producer!

- **BUY IN BULK:** Supermarkets often sell lemons, limes, apples, and avocados in pre-assembled bags. The price of these is usually a lot lower than if you were to buy each item one by one. Don't worry about the larger amount; you'll work your way through a bag of lemons or apples quickly once you start making a green juice every day.

- **CELERY:** Celery is generally a very affordable vegetable. Use a couple of stalks of celery as a base for your green juices and you'll get a lot of bang for your buck.

- **BANANAS:** Bananas tend to turn brown and mushy very quickly. Once you start seeing signs of deterioration, peel the banana and freeze it. Frozen bananas are delicious in smoothies, making them a little more lush and creamy.

- **FLAVORED ICE CUBES:** If you've made a large batch of almond milk that you just know you won't use up before it's too late, freeze half of it in ice-cube trays. These ice cubes will be a great addition to smoothies later. The same goes for coconut water, coconut milk, or any other nut milk.

SMOOTHIE BASES

To make a creamy and delicious smoothie we need to add something liquid to the blender too! While plain water is totally fine, and will do the trick, there is a whole range of other options that also add nice richness, taste, and, most importantly, nutrients. Here are some of my go-to favorites that you'll also see showing up in the recipes throughout the book.

Nut Milk

Nut milks contain a nice dose of healthy fat, protein, vitamins, and minerals and are excellent for using in smoothies. Cashews are high in vitamin B, while Brazil nuts are one of the best sources of selenium. Almond milk contains plenty of vitamin E and calcium. Coconut milk contains lauric acid, which has antibacterial, antiviral, and antifungal benefits. I honestly prefer the taste of nut milks to regular cow's milk!

There's a variety of nut and seed milks on the market now. I personally prefer almond and coconut milk, but feel free to play around and replace the nut milk variety suggested in each recipe with your own favorite, or whatever you happen to have on hand. When buying these milks at the supermarket, make sure to look for an unsweetened variety, and if you can find it, organic is always best. Also, if you have any digestive issues or find yourself sensitive to a lot of foods, you might want to stay clear of carrageenan, a common additive in most

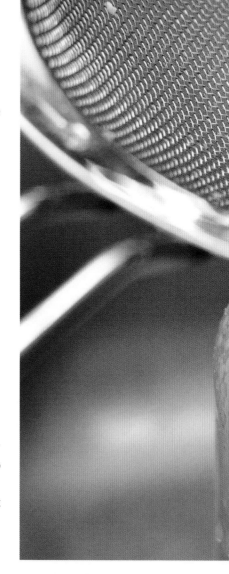

nut milks. I prefer to make my own nut milk, and it's a lot easier than it sounds. Almonds, cashews, hazelnuts, and Brazil nuts all work well.

Coconut Milk

Coconut milk is quite different from the other nut milks. Coconut milk is made by blending the meat of the coconut with the water inside the nuts. Coconut milk used to be available only in a can, but now you can find a thinner version in cartons along with all the other dairy-free milk alternatives. Both kinds are great for using in smoothies. The coconut milk from a can is thicker and more concentrated and therefore also contains more calories and fat. But fear not, this fat is good for you. In fact, it has been shown to aid weight loss. The fatty acids in coconut milk are medium-chain triglycerides and burn faster than other fats. These fatty acids get converted to energy in the liver instead of being stored as fat in the body.

In most of my recipes I use coconut milk from cartons, as it is a bit thinner and works better in smoothies. However, if you can only find canned coconut milk, or you prefer it, you can use it in any recipe. Just dilute the thicker coconut milk with a bit of water. For example, if the recipe calls for 1 cup coconut milk, substitute a mixture of ½ cup canned coconut milk and ½ cup water.

Coconut Water

Coconut water has a naturally sweet taste and is great for adding some additional sweetness and hydration to your drinks. Coconut water is high in electrolytes (potassium and sodium) and has been called nature's own sports drink exactly for that reason. It can help fight off muscle cramps and dehydration. Coconut water is high in potassium—an important nutrient for heart health and regulating blood pressure. Whenever possible, make sure to get raw, unpasteurized coconut water, or even better, water from a fresh, young coconut (the ones with the white, stringy shells). The pasteurization process, used in most bottled or canned coconut water, kills most of the naturally occurring enzymes in the water. I love using coconut water as a base in my really green shakes for a little added sweetness. However, if your drink already contains a lot of sweet fruits, I would avoid adding even more sweetness through coconut water.

DIY NUT MILK

- 1 cup nuts
- 3 cups pure water, plus more for soaking
- Pinch of sea salt
- ½ tsp vanilla extract (optional)
- 2 medjool dates (optional)

Soak nuts of your choice in pure water (I use filtered tap water) overnight or for 6 to 8 hours. Drain and discard the water and rinse the nuts well. Add nuts to the blender and add 3 cups fresh, pure water and a pinch of sea salt. Blend well until the nuts are completely puréed and turned into a white liquid. Strain the blended nuts and water through a very fine mesh strainer, nut-milk bag, triple-folded cheesecloth, or even a (clean!) sock. Now you're left with a pile of nut pulp on one end and a smooth "milk" on the other. Voilà!

If you want to add a little flavor to the milk, return the milk to the blender with a capful of vanilla extract and 2 medjool dates (or regular dates will do just fine) and blend again. You can also blend the milk with some raw cacao powder to make chocolate milk. Yum!

YOU ARE YOUR BEST HEALER

There are a lot of tips, tricks, and well-meaning advice out there. The more you dive into this world of wellness, the more information you'll find. And chances are that one person's recommendation is the same thing another person will warn you to avoid. Fear not! Every body is different and you will learn to listen to your  body and find the foods that truly work for you, your lifestyle, and your body. One person's fuel is another person's poison. While dairy can be a nurturing food for some, we know it's a real troublemaker for others. And while some people thrive on a diet full of raw fruits and vegetables, others do better with more animal proteins and warm foods.

I believe that the location and climate where we live, our lifestyle, stress levels, and even ancestry impact what foods we should eat and what will help us thrive. For example, I live in New York City and the winters here can be long and cold. It does not make much sense for me to be eating or drinking a lot of raw, tropical fruits such as banana and pineapple in January. At that time of year my body needs more warming, hearty foods like fats, whole grains, and protein. But don't get me wrong—it doesn't mean that I can't drink my green drinks! It just means that I'd be better off choosing drinks with more root vegetables, kale, and ginger. Another aspect is ancestry. What did your parents and grandparents eat traditionally? I grew up in Norway, where dairy, fish, and whole grains are all very common foods. Chances are I might tolerate, and even thrive, on a diet that contains some dairy. However, if my ancestors were from a tropical island or Japan, chances are they never ate dairy, nor ever saw a cow or goat in their lives, and that I probably won't thrive on dairy either. This is all pretty common sense and intuitive once we allow ourselves to look at food this way, and not just listen to the latest fad diet out there.

What's true for all of us is that real, whole foods, as close to nature as possible, whether animal foods or plants, are the most nurturing, healing, and nourishing for our bodies. And greens certainly fall under that category!

Herbal Tea and Green Tea

Have you ever thought of using tea in your smoothies? It can be a nutritious and delicious addition. Fruity and flowery herbal teas such as hibiscus, rose hip, and tropical blends work well, as well as green tea and matcha green tea. Hibiscus is a flower known for its blood pressure–lowering abilities. The tea from this dried flower has a deep red color and slightly sour and flowery taste. Rose hip contains a good dose of vitamin C and has stomach-soothing benefits too. Green tea and especially matcha (a high-quality green tea powder) is high in antioxidants, and the caffeine adds a little energy boost. In general, tea has a slightly bitter flavor and works best when used alongside fruit in smoothies. Matcha green tea works especially well with nut milks as a creamy, delicious drink.

Fruit Juice

Fruit juice can be used as a liquid base for your smoothies. Grapefruit, orange, and apple juice work well, but watch out—they are high in naturally occurring sugar. Cranberry, cherry, blueberry, and black currant juices are high in antioxidants and also work well, especially in smoothies where you are also adding these berries whole. Ideally, use freshly made juices instead of the pasteurized or from-concentrate juices found at the supermarket.

PART TWO

GREEN DRINK RECIPES

DETOX / 73

RECHARGE / 107

VITALITY / 129

ENERGY / 163

DIGESTION / 183

FOR GOOD MEASURE

A few words about measuring: The recipes in this book all include suggested measurements for each ingredient. Just keep in mind that an apple is not an apple—some apples are large, some are small, some are sweet, and others are tart. Therefore, no one drink will taste exactly the same each time you make it, and really, that's part of the fun and appeal! Making smoothies is not like baking, and you really don't have to measure out every ingredient exactly. You can simply "eyeball" the measurements and even add more of the ingredients you love and less of the stuff you don't. Customize each drink to your liking and if you don't have one of the required ingredients on hand, don't worry—just switch it out for something similar. Don't have any pears? Use apple. Don't have romaine lettuce? Use spinach! Ran out of blueberries? Well, blackberries will do just fine. You get the idea.

Along those lines, the amount of juice or smoothie is also variable. You should get about 16 ounces of juice for each recipe, a good size for one person or even enough to share if you're so inclined.

detox

Even if we do our best with our own diets and our own homes, we inevitably get exposed to environmental toxins from the air we breathe, the water we drink, and, yes, even the food we eat. Our bodies can handle some of it, but once it gets overwhelmed and the liver has too much work to do, we start feeling sluggish, tired, and unwell. That's when it's time to lighten the load and do some internal cleansing.

By switching to smoothies and juices as our main source of nutrients for a few days, we take the pressure off our digestive system, which can then deal with some of the built-up problems it hasn't been able to attend to for a while. The juices help provide an instant nutrient boost and support for the liver to do its job. The smoothies, although blended well, still provide fiber, which helps sweep the intestine clean, keeps the bowels regular, and helps move the toxins out of the body once they've been processed by the liver. We know that our liver needs protein to properly detox, so it's good to include some easily digestible pea protein powder (or another vegan protein that you like) in your shakes a few times a day.

I have also included some recipes in this section that are low in sugar and fruit. Fruit is loaded with nutrients that are good for us, but for people with yeast overgrowth (such as candida) the naturally occurring sugar in fruit can be a problem. The yeast feeds on sugar, so the more sugar we feed it, the harder it is to get rid of it. These low- or no-sugar recipes are great for anyone to enjoy, whether you're on a cleanse, dealing with yeast, or not. I personally love my green juices slightly tart anyway!

immunity
green smoothie

This drink is packed with hydrating and immune-boosting properties, without too much sweetness and sugar that can compromise an already weakened immune system. Ginger is known for its anti-inflammatory properties and is a great digestive aid, while the probiotics add healthy bacteria to your gut. Despite their acidic taste, lemons are alkaline forming in the body and contain a good dose of antioxidants and vitamin C. Drink up and you'll be fit to fight!

1 cup coconut water

2 leaves romaine lettuce

½ green apple (such as Granny Smith)

¼ cucumber

¼ avocado, peeled

½ lemon, peeled

½-inch slice fresh ginger

½ cup fresh parsley

1 serving probiotic powder or the contents of a probiotic capsule (follow instructions on the bottle)

3–4 ice cubes (optional)

Add all ingredients to the blender, except ice. If you have a high-speed blender you can leave the peel and core on the apple and cucumber. If not, you might want to remove them. Blend on high until all the ingredients have turned into a smooth liquid. Add ice cubes (if using) and blend for another 10 seconds. Serve and enjoy!

bittersweet symphony

A detox can be bittersweet sometimes. The moments of not indulging in our guilty pleasure can be both sad and rewarding all at once. So in honor of all things detox, here is a nutritious green smoothie with bitter grapefruit, rewarding greens, and sweet, sweet honey!

1 cup water

½ grapefruit, peeled

1 cup or 4 large leaves romaine lettuce

1 tbsp raw honey

Add all ingredients to the blender and blend well.

✳ RAW HONEY BOOSTER

You might think of honey as just another sweetener, but honey has a lot to offer beyond its sweet taste. Raw honey is a whole and natural food, as opposed to processed white sugar. Honey also has antibacterial and antiviral properties and supports our immune system. It even contains antioxidants and can help reduce inflammation. I prefer using raw and local honey, which can also act as a booster to fight off seasonal allergy symptoms.

coconut greens

I love sipping fresh coconut water out of the nut! It brings me straight to a Caribbean beach, feeling my toes in the sand and the sea breeze in my hair. So, when I need to be transported away from busy New York, just for a few moments, this drink really does the trick. Just close your eyes and imagine . . .

1 whole young coconut

1 cup or 1 big handful mini kale (or substitute spinach)

3 ice cubes

Hack open the coconut and pour all the liquid inside it straight into your blender. Scoop out the meat from the coconut (a melon baller works well, but any spoon will do) and add the meat to the blender. Add kale and blend until everything is well mixed. Stop the blender, add the ice, and blend again for another 20 seconds or so. Sip slowly with a straw and dream your way to a tropical beach.

pineapple greens

This is a super refreshing, light, and hydrating summer drink packed with enzymes and electrolytes. The romaine provides a little dose of protein too, making this a great, light snack.

1½ cups coconut water

1 cup chopped pineapple, peeled and cored

½ cucumber

1 cup or 3–4 leaves romaine lettuce

3 ice cubes

Add all ingredients to the blender, except ice. Blend until all the ingredients have turned into a smooth liquid. Add the ice cubes and blend for another 10 seconds or until the ice is crushed and well blended into the drink.

grapefruit greens

I love grapefruit as part of my breakfast, so here I've added it to a luscious green smoothie! Lime and cilantro give this drink an exotic flair, and with grapefruit and lime as the only fruits, this is a drink that's also very low in sugar.

1 cup water

1 cup or 4 large leaves romaine lettuce

1 stalk celery

⅓ cucumber

½ grapefruit, peeled

½ lime, peeled

⅓ cup cilantro

Add all ingredients to the blender and blend well.

✳ CILANTRO BOOSTER

Cilantro has so much more to offer than its controversial taste (either you love it or you hate it). This is a detoxing herb that helps chelate toxic metals from the body. Now that is one powerful herb! It also acts as a natural antiseptic and can help wounds heal. This delicious herb is also rich in minerals, including iron and magnesium—two minerals many of us lack. So if you're among us cilantro lovers, drink up! And if you're a hater, substitute parsley.

refresh smoothie

If you're looking for a light and refreshing drink without too much sugar, this is the one. The Refresh Smoothie would make for a perfect pre-workout snack because it's packed with electrolyte power from the coconut water and replenishing minerals from the greens.

1½ cups coconut water

½ cup kale

½ cup spinach

½ cup romaine lettuce

½ lime, peeled

Leaves from 2 stems of mint

Add all ingredients to the blender and blend well.

green power bliss

On a detox we still need healthy fats, protein, and fiber! I use pea protein here because when you're detoxing, it's nice to choose the most easily digestible and gentle proteins possible. The chia seeds add fiber to keep you all sorts of regular, and there's plenty of sweetness from coconut and pear to make this an absolute crowd-pleaser.

1 cup almond milk

½ pear

¼ avocado, peeled

1 packed cup spinach

¼ cup coconut water

1 tsp chia seeds

1 scoop pea protein powder (or substitute hemp or brown rice protein)

1 cup pure water (or less or more if desired)

Blend all ingredients, except water, until smooth. Then put the blender on slow and pour in water until the smoothie reaches desired consistency. You can make it so thick you'll eat it with a spoon, or as thin as a juice.

oj & greens

This is a potent anti-inflammatory drink packed with the antioxidants beta-carotene and vitamin C! It will do wonders for aching joints and boost your immune system during the cold and flu season.

2 oranges (or 1 cup freshly squeezed orange juice)

1 carrot

1-inch slice fresh ginger

1-inch slice fresh turmeric or ¼ tsp turmeric powder

½ lemon, peeled

1 tbsp raw honey

1 cup or 4 leaves romaine lettuce

Start by squeezing the oranges to create 1 cup orange juice. Add the juice and the remaining ingredients to the blender and blend very well until everything is smooth. Serve at room temperature or pour over a few ice cubes if you prefer.

 **✳ CARROT BOOSTER**

Carrots are high in the antioxidant beta-carotene, also known as vitamin A. When you slice a carrot you notice a perfect circle at the core—it looks like a human eye! And wouldn't you know it—carrots are great for eyesight.

greenest green

This is for the dedicated and, dare I say, more advanced green drink drinkers. Without any sweet fruits, this drink is as green as they get, yet refreshing and deliciously cleansing.

1½ cups water

1 stalk celery

½ cucumber

½ avocado

1 cup or 4 leaves romaine lettuce

⅓ cup parsley

½ lemon, peeled

Pinch of sea salt

Add all ingredients to the blender and blend very well.

 **AVOCADO BOOSTER**

Also known as an alligator pear, the avocado is actually not a vegetable but a fruit, and contains about 20 percent fat, more than any other fruit. Avocados are loaded with vitamin E and great for protecting both our skin and our heart. Their high level of oleic acid—a fatty acid—can help lower bad cholesterol (LDL). And did you know avocados actually contain the same amount of potassium as two to three bananas?

the green master

Have you ever considered doing the hard-core cleanse known as the Master Cleanse? Well, I've done it, and I do not recommend it to anyone. It puts your body in starvation mode, which makes you gain back all the weight you lose and then some. Also, for most of us this kind of extreme detoxing ends up dumping too many toxins on our poor liver at once. Instead, add this drink to your healthy-habit regimen. It's packed with cleansing nutrients and fiber to help sweep you clean.

1 cup or 3 leaves kale

¼ green apple

½ lemon, peeled

1-inch slice fresh ginger

¼ tsp cayenne pepper

1 tbsp real maple syrup

½ cup water

½ cup freshly made apple juice

Add all ingredients to your blender, pouring the liquids over the top. Blend until everything is smoothly mixed. Sip it slowly!

✳ CAYENNE BOOSTER

Cayenne pepper helps increase circulation, which is an important aspect of a successful cleanse. This spicy pepper also breaks up mucus in the body, helping dissolve and release toxic buildup. It can also heat up the body and therefore boost the metabolism.

dandelion detox

Whenever we are detoxing we have to make sure to look after the liver—the body's main detoxing organ. It is hard at work processing all the toxins that enter our body, whether we like it or not. This smoothie should provide your hardworking liver with some well-deserved fuel!

1½ cups coconut water

¼ avocado, peeled

1 cup dandelion greens

½ cup frozen blueberries

1 tbsp raw cacao powder

1 tbsp hemp powder or seeds

Add all ingredients to the blender and blend well.

✳ DANDELION BOOSTER

This bitter, green, and wild leaf is packed with minerals, including calcium and iron, of which so many of us need more. Dandelion is also packed with antioxidants and chlorophyll. What makes dandelion different from the other leafy greens (and I love 'em all!) is that it's wild. It's easily found in nature or in your own garden, which makes it free! Wild weeds also carry a unique energy of, well, let's call it fierceness!

dandelion bliss

This smoothie is hydrating and a little tart, with just a touch of sweetness. Dandelion is a powerful wild weed with a slightly bitter taste, so the apple and lemon help round out the flavors nicely.

1 cup water

1 cup chopped cucumber

1 cup dandelion greens

½ green apple

½ lemon, peeled

Add all ingredients to the blender and blend very well.

fall into winter greens

This is a fall- and winter-friendly recipe packed with fiber and flavor. Fennel adds a slight licorice taste, and pear adds just enough juicy, honey-sweet flavor. Bosc pears work well in smoothies; they are usually a little more soft and juicy. Kale is a great wintery green and usually available year-round.

1 cup water (or more if needed)
⅓ bulb fennel
1 cup or 3 leaves kale (stems removed)
½ pear

Add all ingredients to the blender and blend well.

✳ FENNEL BOOSTER

Fennel contains oils that help relieve cramps and spasms in the digestive tract. These oils can even help dispel gas to ease uncomfortable bloating.

green goddess smoothie

This is a great, light breakfast option when you're doing a little internal cleansing. Pineapple contains natural enzymes, and cilantro is a natural chelator that helps draw out and get rid of toxins. And all the fiber from the greens helps finish the job.

1 cup coconut water

1 cup chopped pineapple, peeled and cored

3 leaves romaine lettuce

2 leaves kale

½ lime, peeled

¼ cup cilantro

Add all ingredients to the blender and blend well.

jicama-cilantro slush

This is a smoothie very low in sugar yet very high in nutritional value. The starchy tuber jicama and the fatty avocado make this drink nice and creamy, while the cilantro and lime add a powerful detox effect.

1 cup peeled and cubed jicama

¼ cucumber, cubed

¼ cup cilantro

¼ avocado, peeled

½ lime, peeled

Add all ingredients to the blender and blend well.

* JICAMA BOOSTER

Jicama is a tuber, just like yam, and is high in carbohydrates. It tastes slightly sweet but is crunchy like a water chestnut. It is native to Mexico but has now spread to Asia too; you often find it in Vietnamese cuisine. Jicama is packed with dietary fiber to help move things along and prevent blood sugar spikes. It has plenty of potassium, a mineral many of us don't get enough of, as well as vitamins C, A, and B. I'll drink to that!

cilantro fiesta juice

Cilantro makes me happy! This juice is ready to party, and if you're opting out of the margaritas for a while, it makes for a very good substitute.

6 leaves romaine lettuce

½ cup cilantro

½ lime, peeled

1½ cups chopped pineapple, peeled and cored

Put all the ingredients through a juicer. Alternate between the pineapple and romaine to help move everything through smoothly.

all greens juice

All greens, all good! This juice is nicely tart and very green, in the best ways possible. Without any added sweet fruits, this is a great choice for anyone who wants to cut back on all sugars and still drink their juice.

4 stalks celery

½ cucumber

2 leaves kale

1 leaf chard, any variety (with stem)

1 handful of spinach

½ cup parsley

½ lemon, peeled

1-inch slice fresh ginger (or more if you like it hot!)

Put all the ingredients through a juicer. Alternate between harder foods, like celery and cucumber, and the leafy greens to help move everything through smoothly.

 **GINGER BOOSTER**

Ginger is one of the absolute most powerful anti-inflammatory agents out there. It is even used to relieve the symptoms of arthritis and osteoporosis. Ginger has also been shown to decrease muscle pain and soothe stomachaches, nausea, and flatulence. Bonus: Ginger has been celebrated as an aphrodisiac for centuries. So go ahead and turn up the heat!

beet it juice

Boost your detox with some potent and bright beet juice. I love the pretty color of beets and their sweet and earthy flavor. The ginger adds a kick and some anti-inflammatory benefits. The lemon makes it all come together. And don't worry; I didn't forget about the greens either. A cup of kale should round things off perfectly. To good health!

2 beets

1 lemon, peeled

1½-inch slice fresh ginger

1 carrot

1 cup or 3 leaves kale (stems included)

Put all the ingredients through a juicer. Alternate between harder foods, like beets and carrots, and kale to help move everything through smoothly.

✳ BEET BOOSTER

As you can see from the beet's incredibly bright color, this root vegetable is loaded with antioxidants. The purple pigment in beets is called betacyanin and can have great liver benefits—it actually helps increase the level of detoxifying enzymes in the liver. This certainly makes beet juice the perfect hangover helper! Recent studies are also confirming that beets can have a nice blood pressure-lowering effect. So, go ahead and chill out with a glass of beet juice.

green monster juice

When I grab a green juice at a juice bar in the city, this is usually what I ask them to make. Yes, it's very green, but with just enough apple and lemon to make it absolutely delicious. Every single ingredient helps boost detoxification and provides your body with a multitude of micronutrients.

1 stalk celery

2 leaves kale

4 leaves romaine lettuce

½ cucumber

½ apple

½ lemon, peeled

2 stems parsley

Put all the ingredients through a juicer. Alternate between harder foods, like celery and cucumber, and the leafy greens and herbs to help move everything through smoothly.

 APPLE
BOOSTER

Apples are a great source of pectin, a soluble fiber that has been shown to help lower bad cholesterol (LDL). Apples contain lots of flavonoids that help protect our body against heart disease. There is also research pointing to apples' ability to stabilize blood sugar and our healthy gut flora. Apples have great cleansing properties, especially when consumed in the fall, helping our bodies expel excess heat and cool down before winter.

recharge

ometimes we need a little extra love. We've worked out hard and need to refuel, or we're a little under the weather and need to slow things down, take a break, and drink some healing tonic. In this chapter I've gathered recipes that are perfect for those times when you need to recharge your batteries. Whether you are feeling fatigued and depleted or just in need of some tender loving care, you will find a nourishing drink for yourself here.

Many of the drinks in this chapter have some added protein and are perfect after a hard workout session or a long hike. Others are boosted with a little honey and ginger to fight off a stubborn cold. There are also great breakfast-of-champions smoothies in this chapter for those days when you know you're going to need that little extra (and maybe for you, that's every day!). With protein, vitamins, minerals, and fats, many of these drinks even work well as a complete meal.

Kick back, sip slowly, and recharge the batteries.

c booster

Feeling a little under the weather? Well, I've got just the right elixir for you. This smoothie is packed with vitamin C and anti-inflammatory ginger as well as honey, which has powerful antimicrobial properties. Nip that cold in the bud once and for all.

1 orange, peeled and seeded

1 cup kale

½ lemon, peeled

1 tbsp raw honey

1-inch slice fresh ginger, grated into the blender

Add all ingredients to the blender and blend well.

✳ ORANGE BOOSTER

Oranges have long been celebrated for their high vitamin C content. Vitamin C is an antioxidant that helps protect our cells from free-radical damage and so it's a serious cancer fighter! Oranges are also high in potassium, an electrolyte that protects our heart and helps prevent muscle cramping. Since oranges are pretty sweet and high in sugar, I prefer to eat them whole or blended into smoothies to maintain all the fiber intact.

copacabana

If you feel passionate about coconut's deliciousness, you're going to love this drink. It's so incredibly simple, refreshing, and delicious—you wouldn't know there was anything healthy about it. But there is! Coconut's water and flesh contain potassium and healthy fats that help restore lost fluids and energy. No wonder it's the one food easily available on desert islands.

1 whole coconut

1 cup spinach

1 frozen banana

Hack open the coconut and pour all the water inside straight into your blender. Scoop out the meat from the coconut (a melon baller works really well, but any spoon will do) and add the meat to your blender. Add spinach and frozen banana and blend it all up.

seeds of change

This is a creamy, rich, and immensely satisfying shake packed with healthy fats. This shake may just change your life for the better.

1 cup almond milk (homemade is best)

1 tbsp hemp seeds

1 tbsp flax seeds

1 tbsp chia seeds

1-inch slice fresh ginger

1 cup spinach

1 frozen banana

Add all ingredients to the blender and blend well.

açai green

I love this smoothie! It's refreshing, energizing, and packed with antioxidants. The added fats and protein also make this one an easy meal replacement, especially for breakfast. You can make it thicker by using a little less liquid and serve it in a bowl with a sprinkle of your favorite seeds, coconut flakes, and fresh berries.

1½ cups almond milk

½ cup blueberries

1 pack (about 3.5 oz) frozen unsweetened açai

1 cup spinach

¼ avocado, peeled

1 tsp chia seeds

1 scoop pea protein (or other protein of choice)

Place all ingredients in a blender, blend everything well, and sip it slowly.

power breakfast

Yum! This is a whole breakfast meal blended into one delicious shake. Pour it into a jar and take it to go, or make it so thick and luscious that you can eat it with a spoon. The green tea and fiber should keep you full and fueled for hours!

1 cup cold green tea (unsweetened)

¾ cup kale

½ cup frozen blueberries

⅓ cup rolled oats

½ banana

1 medjool date or 1 tbsp honey (optional)

Add all ingredients to the blender, except the date or honey, and blend well. Taste for sweetness and add a little honey or a date if you like your breakfast a little sweeter.

✱ BLUEBERRY BOOSTER

Blueberries are one of my favorite smoothie ingredients! They are high in antioxidants and fiber, yet low in sugar. Blueberries are loaded with flavonoids, the antioxidants that are also responsible for their blue-purple color. These potent little berries contain a good amount of vitamin C as well as compounds that help protect against urinary tract infections.

purple & green

This is one of my all-time favorite, go-to recipes. It is a great breakfast shake, but also does wonders after a tough workout. I love the little cinnamon touch, and the avocado makes it rich and creamy without adding lots of extra sugar.

1 cup coconut milk

½ cup fresh or frozen blueberries

1 cup spinach

½ tsp cinnamon

¼ avocado

1 scoop pea protein

Water (optional)

Add all the ingredients to the blender, except water, and blend well. Some protein powders thicken the drink, so you might need some additional water. Check the consistency before adding any extra liquid. It's easy to add more water to make a drink thinner, but not so easy to make a drink thicker if it's too thin.

whey to go!

This shake provides your body with healing superfuel to help you recharge the batteries and restore your muscles after some heavy lifting, long-distance running, or a tough day. Whey (pun intended!) better than anything you can buy!

1 cup nut milk of your choice

½ cup frozen berries (blueberries or mixed berries)

1 cup kale

1 scoop chocolate-flavored whey

1 tbsp raw cocoa powder

3 drops liquid stevia

3 ice cubes

Add all the ingredients to the blender, except ice. Blend well, then add ice and blend for another few seconds.

pb & jelly

Chances are the kid in you still loves a peanut butter and jelly sandwich and a milk-shake. Well, here you've got it all in one healthy concoction! Nut butter loaded with healthy fats and antioxidant-packed raspberries—all in a creamy shake!

1 cup almond milk

1 tbsp almond butter (or substitute peanut butter)

1 cup frozen raspberries

1 cup spinach

1 scoop vanilla pea protein

1 tbsp maple syrup (optional)

Add all ingredients to the blender, except maple syrup, and blend well. Taste test before adding the maple syrup. You may not even need it!

winter wonder

This is true comfort food, packed with warming and sweet winter spices and persimmon—a bright orange winter fruit with a delicious sweet taste.

1 cup almond milk

1 persimmon

1 cup or 1 handful of spinach

½ tsp cinnamon

¼ tsp cardamom

½ tsp vanilla extract

1 medjool date

Add all ingredients to the blender and blend well.

✳ PERSIMMON BOOSTER

I didn't grow up eating persimmon, or ever even tasting it, so to me it's an exotic fruit. I love its bright orange color and the glossy skin—not to mention its supersweet and luscious flesh. Persimmons contain pectin, a fiber that helps regulate blood sugar and lower LDL cholesterol. So, despite its sweet flavor, it contains enough fiber to curb cravings and keep you feeling full for longer. It is also rich in minerals and high in antioxidants and both vitamins C and A.

jessica rabbit juice

Carrot juice is a true and trusted staple, but have you ever tried it mixed with kale and olive oil? The olive oil doesn't just add a nice flavor, it also aids the absorption of the fat-soluble vitamins!

3 carrots

½ apple

1 cup kale or chard

½-inch slice fresh ginger

½ tbsp olive oil

Put all ingredients through a juicer, except olive oil. Alternate between harder foods, like apple and carrots, and kale to help move everything through smoothly. Stir in the olive oil at the end.

"v8" garden juice

This juice tastes quite a bit like a Bloody Mary, so it makes for a great pick-me-up after a fun night of dancing and maybe one too many glasses of your favorite party beverage. It's perfect served in a big pitcher shared at the brunch table with your friends. It is a little sweet, a little salty, and a little spicy—something for everyone.

2 tomatoes

¼ cucumber

½ jalapeño, seeds removed

Handful of parsley

2 stalks celery

½ bulb fennel

1 carrot

½ lemon

Sea salt and fresh pepper to taste

Put all the ingredients through a juicer, except salt and pepper. Alternate between harder foods, like celery and cucumber, and tomatoes and parsley to help move everything through smoothly.

Add a little sea salt and freshly ground pepper. And for full Bloody Mary effect, serve garnished with a celery stick, two green olives, and a slice of lemon.

✳ JALAPEÑO BOOSTER

Jalapeños are rich in potassium, which helps fight muscle cramping—perfect after a long night of dancing. They also contain capsaicin, which is believed to boost metabolism. Spicy foods in general help curb the appetite slightly and speed up the metabolism, so hot peppers can be helpful for people trying to lose weight.

vitality

Looking for an overall uplifting boost of well-being? Well, then this chapter is packed with recipes for you. Longevity is about more than just living longer—it's about improved quality of life! And quality is all about healthy, nutritious food and delicious flavor. I sure would rather have my healthy food also taste good. Wouldn't you? Delicious food brings us pleasure, joy, and satisfaction—all good things to experience as often as possible. So, here you'll find a variety of delicious, refreshing, and wellness-boosting recipes.

And did I mention that these drinks also bring with them some fantastic benefits for your skin? They are jam-packed with antioxidants—the powerful free-radical warriors that help fight skin-cell damage from sun and pollution! The healthy fats from avocados, coconuts, and almonds, added to many of the drinks in this chapter, help to moisturize your skin from within. And the collagen boost you'll get from consuming plenty of vitamin C from both the greens and citrus is better than any antiaging cream I've ever tried.

Cheers to good health and a long, rich life filled with joy!

Peachy Green

Summer peaches are oh-so-sweet and delicious, but their season is oh-so-short. Make sure to take advantage of it while it lasts. Make this refreshing and simple summer drink packed with vitamin C and peachy goodness!

½ cup coconut milk

Juice of 1 orange

1 peach (pit removed)

1 cup or 4 large leaves romaine lettuce

Add all ingredients to the blender and blend well.

✳ PEACH BOOSTER

Peaches contain carotenes and flavonoids, antioxidants that help prevent degeneration and protect us against cancer. Peaches contain plenty of skin-boosting vitamin C. They also contain a lot of fiber and potassium, which can help reduce kidney-related problems. And best of all, they're one of the most delicious fruits out there. No candy needed!

hail to
the kale

Are you still scared of kale? This smoothie will finally make you a convert. With avocado for creaminess and pear for sweetness, the kale's slightly bitter flavor completely disappears. But the benefits are still there: minerals, and vitamins A, C, and K, plus forty-five different antioxidants to help your body fight off free radicals. Enough said!

1 cup coconut water

1 cup kale

½ pear

¼ avocado, peeled

½ cucumber

½ lemon, peeled

Handful of cilantro

½-inch slice ginger

1 scoop protein powder (such as hemp or pea)

½–1 cup water, as needed to reach desired consistency

Add all ingredients to the blender, except the water, and blend well. Check the consistency and add a little more water if needed.

✳ KALE BOOSTER

Curly kale, ornamental kale, purple kale, dinosaur kale, lacinato kale: many varieties and names, one incredibly healthy vegetable. In fact, kale is one of the most nutrient-dense vegetables. Kale is very high in chlorophyll and carotenes. It's also packed with calcium, making it a great vegetable for our bones. Kale, as well as all other members of the cabbage family, has anticancer properties.

kiwi, spinach & avocado

This smoothie is creamy, green, slightly sweet, and a little sour, yet very low in sugar! It's an excellent afternoon snack with vitamin C, healthy fat, and hydrating electrolytes to keep you charged for the whole afternoon.

1½ cups coconut water

1 cup spinach

2 kiwis, peeled

½ avocado, peeled

Add all ingredients to the blender and blend well. For an even more filling and boosting drink, add a scoop of plain or vanilla-flavored pea protein powder.

✳ KIWI BOOSTER

Kiwi is high in vitamin C for skin health and immunity, and potassium for sodium balance. It also contains the enzyme actinidain, which helps with the digestion of protein. Kiwi is one of the fruits lowest in sugar and highest in fiber, so you won't get the insulin rush you might experience from some other fruits.

apple pie

There is something incredibly comforting about a piece of homema
I took all that warm goodness and transformed it into a smoothie perfect for you,
with walnuts, apples, and cinnamon. And, of course, a handful of kale for good
measure.

1 apple, peeled

1 cup kale

1 cup nut milk

½ tsp cinnamon

¼ lemon, peeled

¼ cup walnuts

Add all ingredients to the blender and blend well.

✳ WALNUT BOOSTER

Take a close look at a shelled walnut. Does it remind you of something? It looks like a little brain! And go figure—this nut is loaded with brain food in the form of omega-3 fatty acids. Omega-3s also help fight inflammation and balance the cholesterol in the body. Walnuts also contain vitamin E, which has a slight blood-thinning effect and can help protect against strokes and heart attacks.

sweet almond kale

This creamy and sweet smoothie feels like nothing less than an indulgence. Yet it packs a real nutritional punch! Almonds are rich in vitamin E (an antioxidant) and contain a good dose of monounsaturated fats, which help keep your heart healthy. Kale is king, with forty-five different antioxidants to help fight cancer.

1 cup kale

1½ cups almond milk

½ banana (fresh or frozen)

½ cup mango (fresh or frozen)

1 tbsp raw, unsalted almond butter

¼ tsp cinnamon

Add kale to the blender and add the almond milk. Blend for a few seconds before adding remaining ingredients. Blend everything together for about 30 seconds, or until you have a smooth drink. Cheers!

✳ CINNAMON BOOSTER

You may think cinnamon is just another holiday cookie ingredient, but did you know this potent brown bark also helps fight inflammation? In fact, cinnamon has been shown to help lower blood sugar and bad cholesterol. Chinese medicine also describes cinnamon's warming properties—no wonder I love to sprinkle it on everything during the cold winter months.

green mojito

Sometimes all you want is a summery cocktail without the hangover. With this drink you can have your cocktail and drink it too, guilt-free! This is also a perfect crowd pleaser at any summer BBQ. No one will miss the rum.

1 cup water

1 cup chopped pineapple, peeled and cored

½ lime, peeled

1 cup or 1 big handful of spinach

Leaves of 2 stalks (about ¼ cup) mint

6 ice cubes

Add all ingredients to the blender, except the ice, and blend well. Add ice cubes and blend for another few seconds until everything is well mixed.

banana chard

Sweet bananas and tangerines, mixed with hydrating coconut water and Swiss chard! So incredibly simple and yet a total taste explosion! I hope you like it too.

1 cup coconut water

1 banana

1 tangerine, peeled and seeded

1 cup or 2–3 leaves Swiss chard, stems removed

Add all ingredients to the blender and blend well.

morning sun

Rise and shine with this delicious green drink packed with vitamins and minerals for lasting vitality throughout the day. A little orange adds a familiar morning touch, and the nut milk provides satisfying, healthy, and glow-promoting fats!

1 cup nut milk

¼ mango, peeled

1 cup or 3 large leaves kale (stem removed) or any other greens you have on hand

½ banana

½ orange, peeled and seeded

Add all ingredients to the blender and blend well.

frozen
green lemonade

This is as refreshing as it gets! It's frozen, with additional cooling benefits from mint. Lemon and stevia add the perfect sweet and sour balance. Instead of tea, you can also use cold water that has been infused with fresh mint for a few hours.

½ cup chilled mint tea

½ cup spinach

½ cup or 2 leaves romaine lettuce

5 leaves mint

1 lemon, peeled

5 drops or 1 packet stevia

1 cup ice

Add all ingredients, but only ½ cup ice, to the blender and blend well. Then add remaining ice and blend for a few more seconds.

✳ LEMON BOOSTER

Lemons are packed with vitamin C, which is crucial for proper immune function and is a great antioxidant. Lemon also stimulates the liver to detoxify. And no wonder lemonade is the beverage of choice on hot summer days: Lemons are a good source of electrolytes!

mango madness

Mango and greens is a match made in heaven. The juicy sweetness of mango balances out any green taste of the leafy greens. The coconut adds lots of satisfying healthy fats that also aid with the absorption of all the good beta-carotene from the mango!

1 cup water

1 tbsp coconut manna (a mixture of coconut oil and meat)

1 mango, peeled and pit removed
(1 cup frozen mango works too!)

1 cup greens (romaine, spinach, or kale)

⅓ cup cilantro

4 ice cubes

Add all ingredients, except ice, in a blender. If you don't have coconut manna, you can substitute 1 cup coconut milk instead of water and manna.

Blend until nice and smooth, then add ice and blend a few more seconds. Enjoy as soon as possible.

✳ MANGO BOOSTER

Mangos are loaded with nutrients: carotenoids, vitamin C, copper, and vitamin A, to name just a few. They have cancer-preventing properties and can protect against infections, too! Mangos are also rich in enzymes that improve digestion. Their high content of carotenoids makes them a great skin food. No wonder this is one of the most commonly consumed fruits in the world!

northern lights

This smoothie is a humble ode to my Nordic roots. Dairy is a staple in the Norwegian diet, and our summer berries are, dare I say, the best-tasting berries in the world. I spent summers picking and eating sweet cherries next to the fjord. Here I've combined all these sweet memories with a dash of fresh spinach.

½ cup plain goat or sheep's milk yogurt

½ cup water

½ cup frozen mixed berries

½ cup sweet cherries (pits removed)

1 cup baby spinach

1 tbsp raw honey

Add all ingredients to the blender and blend well.

✳ CHERRY BOOSTER

Just like other dark blue or purple fruits, cherries are loaded with flavonoids—antioxidants that help protect us from inflammation and cancer. Cherries have also been found to help relieve symptoms associated with gout—a form of arthritis—by lowering uric acid levels.

red & ready

Cherries are on the top of my list of absolute favorite foods (and the list is long!). Here I've mixed cherries with slightly floral and sour hibiscus tea, and the final result is a beautiful, red, sweet, and tart smoothie. Enjoy!

1 cup cooled hibiscus tea

1 cup sweet cherries (frozen or fresh; pits removed)

1 cup spinach

½ tsp cinnamon

4 ice cubes

Blend everything together, except ice, in a blender. Blend until smooth, then add ice and blend a few more seconds. Pour into a tall red-wine glass for a proper, grown-up experience.

the kiwi

Kiwis are a fun and unexpected addition to smoothies. Here I've mixed kiwi with some creamy avocado, refreshing lime, and, of course, some leafy greens. It makes for a pretty darn delicious green smoothie!

½ cup coconut milk

½ cup coconut water

1 kiwi, peeled

¼ avocado, peeled

Juice of ½ lime

½ cup spinach

3 drops liquid stevia (optional)

Add all ingredients to the blender and blend well.

the
bee-utiful

With both bee pollen and honey, we're harvesting some energizing and immune-boosting powers from our buzzing friends. And did you know bee pollen is 40 percent protein?

1 cup almond milk

½ avocado, peeled

½ cup kale

1 tbsp bee pollen

1 tbsp honey

Add all ingredients to the blender and blend well.

watermelon medley juice

I just love watermelon and mint together. I toss it in my summer salads or serve it as a simple snack. But then I thought, why not blend it all into a juice? So here it is, watermelon, mint, and some green goodness with a little ginger surprise. So incredibly good, it makes me long for a hot summer's day.

1½ cups watermelon

½ cucumber

1 cup kale (3–4 small leaves with stems)

6 leaves mint

1-inch slice fresh ginger

Put all ingredients through a juicer. Alternate between harder foods, like cucumber, and kale and mint to help move everything through smoothly.

✳ WATERMELON BOOSTER

Watermelon, as the name implies, is packed with hydrating water. It's also a diuretic and the perfect food in hot summer weather. Watermelon also contains plenty of antioxidants, including vitamin C.

cucumber cooler juice

This is the juice to serve yourself on a hot summer day or after a sweaty yoga class. Cooling mint and cucumber will hydrate and calm you down, bringing your body right back to its comfort zone in no time.

1½ cucumbers (or 1 English cucumber)

1 lime, peeled

6 leaves mint

Put all the ingredients through a juicer. Sneak the mint leaves in with some cucumber to help them move through the juicer easily.

skin tonic juice

Here's a delicious juice that promotes healthy, dewy, and glowing skin. The cucumber is hydrating and contains silica, known for its amazing skin-toning benefits.

1 cucumber

½ lemon, peeled

1 cup purslane

½ mango, peeled and pit removed

Handful of cilantro

Put all ingredients through a juicer. Alternate between the cucumber, the mango, and the purslane and cilantro to help move everything through smoothly.

✳ PURSLANE BOOSTER

Purslane is a green weed high in essential omega-3 fatty acids. The body does not produce omega-3s on its own and needs to get them through food. Omega-3s help lower inflammation. With skin issues such as acne and eczema, it is important to get enough of this anti-inflammatory fatty acid. This juice is for you!

good
greens juice

This juice is easy, light, and absolutely delicious. I love using romaine in my juices. It has a smooth and delicious flavor that is perfect for anyone who's a little new to the whole green juice craze.

4 leaves romaine lettuce

½ lemon, peeled

½ cucumber

½ apple, peeled

½ cup chopped pineapple, peeled and cored

½ cup basil

Put all the ingredients through a juicer. Alternate between harder foods, like apple, and the pineapple, basil, and romaine to help move everything through smoothly.

energy

All my clients come to me wanting more energy. Our lives are busier than ever, our jobs demand more and more of our time, and yet we still want to have fuel left over to enjoy our friends, family, and (in my case) yoga!

A well-fed and nourished body should be able to enjoy this busy, exciting life without crashing and burning. However, often we are so stretched for time we don't think we have enough time to cook and eat as well as we'd like to. That's exactly why green drinks are so great—they are quick to make, loaded with nutrients, and easy to take with you on the go. I mean, we're talking real fast food here!

I've gathered all my favorite energy-boosting drinks in this next chapter. Some are even boosted with a bit of caffeine from green tea or cacao. And if that, along with all the uplifting and energizing greens, isn't enough, I've also thrown in some energizing superfoods here and there for good measure. So go ahead: blend, chug, work it out, and repeat.

Keep in mind, a well-nourished body is an energized body!

the
green kiss

The avocado adds healthy fat and makes this smoothie super creamy, and the coconut water adds delicious hydrating sweetness. Pear is an underutilized fruit in the smoothie world, but for no good reason. It's deliciously sweet and adds a nice thick and creamy texture.

1 cup coconut water

½ pear

½ avocado, peeled

1 cup spinach

1 tbsp flax seeds

½–1 cup water

Add all ingredients to the blender and blend well. Start by adding just ½ cup water and check the consistency before adding more. Either add enough to make it creamy but drinkable, or keep it lusciously thick and eat it like a pudding.

✳ COCONUT WATER BOOSTER

I love coconut water as a natural, hydrating sports drink on hot and sweaty summer days. Even though I prefer mine straight out of the nut, it's still pretty darn good in this smoothie! Coconut water contains plenty of electrolytes, which help hydrate and restore the body. Its high potassium level also helps relieve hypertension and muscle cramps.

mint chocolate chip shake

I am so thrilled to have come up with this super energizing and cooling shake! Seriously, just try this and I promise, you will never bother to reach for a milkshake or Frappuccino again.

1½ cups almond milk

1 cup spinach

2 tbsp cacao powder (raw is best)

¼ tsp vanilla extract

Leaves from 5 stems mint

5 drops liquid stevia

4 ice cubes

1 tbsp cacao nibs

Blend almond milk, spinach, cacao powder, vanilla, mint, and stevia until smooth. Add ice and blend until crushed, then add cacao nibs and blend for few more seconds. You want the nibs to give you a chocolate chip feeling in the shake, so don't crush them completely.

✳ CACAO BOOSTER

Cacao is the highest antioxidant food on the planet, with tons of magnesium, chromium, iron, and manganese—and most importantly, it's totally delicious! Chocolate can improve cardiovascular health and helps build strong bones. Bonus point: Chocolate leaves us feeling good, too—it is an aphrodisiac and a mood and energy enhancer!

go-go goji

Goji berries are referred to as "happy berries" by Tibetans, who believe that a handful of these bright red berries in the morning will keep you feeling happy all day long. So drink it up and smile like you mean it!

1 cup homemade Brazil nut milk

1 cup or 4 leaves kale

1 banana

½ cup frozen strawberries

1 tbsp goji berries

Add all ingredients to the blender and blend well.

noparadise

...as got it all: sweetness, antioxidant power, healthy fats, complete protein, and deliciousness!

1 cup almond milk

½ cup coconut water

½ banana

½ cup blueberries

1 tbsp coconut manna or butter (coconut oil works fine too)

1 tsp spirulina

1 scoop vanilla protein powder

Add all ingredients to the blender and blend well.

✳ SPIRULINA BOOSTER

Spirulina is one of the few plants that are high in B vitamins, the compounds responsible for turning the food that you need into energy. So if you're running low, fuel up with some spirulina, either in a smoothie like the one above, or in chewable pills to take on the go. Spirulina is about 60 percent pure protein, so it's a great vegan source of complete protein. It is also a good source of GLA, the fat our brain most desires. So, I think it's safe to say we have a real superfood on our hands!

strawberry fields

This smoothie is like a greener, healthier version of strawberries and cream.
And with the added boost of green tea and honey, it will provide you with plenty
of energy! Try it instead of your afternoon coffee.

1 cup coconut milk

1 cup strawberries

⅓ cucumber

½ cup romaine

1 tsp matcha green tea powder

1 tbsp raw honey

Add all ingredients to the blender and blend well.

spiritual gangster

Boost yourself with plenty of hydrating electrolytes and energizing spirulina. Sweet and viscous, nutritious and delicious. Just how I like it!

1½ cups coconut water

1 cup kale

1 banana

10 green grapes

⅓ cucumber

5 mint leaves

1 tsp spirulina

2 ice cubes

Blend everything together, except ice, in a blender. Blend until nice and smooth, then add ice and blend a few more seconds.

matcha shake

This drink is close to a green tea latte, but with even more benefits. Try this shake on a day when you know you need to focus, perform, and deliver!

1 cup almond milk

1 tsp matcha green tea powder

1 frozen banana

1 cup spinach

Stevia to taste (optional)

Add all ingredients to the blender and blend well.

✱ MATCHA BOOSTER

Matcha green tea is a great metabolism booster due to a component called EGCG. As opposed to green tea that you steep, matcha is a finely ground powder, so you actually consume the entire leaf, making it nutritionally superior to other green teas. It is loaded with protective antioxidants and can help fight signs of aging. Matcha green tea also contains caffeine, providing focused energy that can help with performance and concentration.

super brazilian

The combination of Brazil nuts, Amazonian berries, and raw chocolate makes this an exotic, energizing, and nutrient-dense smoothie! The nuts are loaded with selenium, and just a few nuts will cover your daily need. The açai berries are packed with antioxidants, and the cacao provides energy and a little aphrodisiac boost.

1 cup homemade Brazil nut milk

1 tbsp raw cacao powder

1 tsp cacao nibs

1 tsp chia seeds

1 pack açai (about 1 cup)

½ cup spinach

1 medjool date

Add all ingredients to the blender and blend well. Add a little water if needed.

✳ AÇAI BOOSTER

Açai is an antioxidant-rich berry with a deep purple color. One antioxidant in particular, called anthocyanin, is a powerful free-radical fighter. Açai berries also contain fatty acids and together the antioxidants and omega-3s protect the skin and promote a healthy glow. Açai even contains a good amount of protein! Did someone say superfood?

cool it
green juice

Mint and lime make for a perfect combination of cool and refreshing. This juice brings back memories of mojitos at sunset to help you cool off and wind down after a hard day's work.

½ apple, peeled and cored

½ lime, peeled

4 large romaine lettuce leaves

½ cucumber

3 stalks mint

Put all ingredients through a juicer. Alternate between harder foods, like apple and cucumber, and the romaine to help move everything through smoothly.

✳ MINT BOOSTER

Mint symbolizes hospitality and wisdom. It contains oils that help relieve digestive discomforts. Mint helps relax and soothe tense muscles. Mint is also cooling, so enjoy it on a hot summer day, or if you're feeling a bit hot-tempered.

kale
energizer juice

Here we're talking some serious energy boosting! All the kale in this juice might make you feel like you've just had an IV vitamin injection. Vitamins, enzymes, and minerals—it's all there, with the smooth flavor of apple to tie it all together.

2 cups kale

½ yellow apple, peeled and cored

⅓ cucumber

1 stalk celery

½ lemon, peeled

Put all ingredients through a juicer. Alternate between harder foods, like apple and cucumber, and kale to help move everything through smoothly.

digestion

Our digestive systems are incredibly important to our overall health and well-being. The digestive system is responsible for breaking down the food that we eat into fuel for our cells and getting rid of toxins. A well-functioning digestive system should technically not be felt at all—it should just be doing its thing quietly while we go about living our lives. However, for most of us this is not how we feel. I have yet to meet a client who doesn't experience some constipation, bloating, discomfort, gas, and/or heartburn. So what gives?

Due to the common use of antibiotics, found in our food and prescribed as medication, the balance of our intestinal flora can be disturbed. Without enough good bacteria in our gut, we are more susceptible to overgrowth of bad bacteria, fungus, and yeast, as well as being more likely to develop food sensitivities and all kinds of digestive problems.

Whether you're looking for some relief after a less-than-healthy meal, or would like to boost your gut flora, this chapter's for you. Probiotics are the good gut bacteria and can be found in fermented foods such as yogurt, kefir (both dairy and coconut varieties), and pickled vegetables (don't worry—I didn't create a smoothie with sauerkraut!). Adding these foods to your diet, as well as taking a probiotic supplement, is a great preventative measure as well as treatment for digestive problems. The good bacteria also need the right fuel, and getting enough prebiotic foods is crucial for a healthy gut—think fiber-rich foods like fruits and vegetables. Good thing the smoothies in this book are all loaded with that!

Some fruits (pineapple and papaya in particular) contain useful enzymes that can help us digest protein better, so I've included some drinks with these ingredients, too. I've also come up with some delicious drinks with soothing stomach benefits from ingredients such as mint, fennel, and ginger.

So go ahead—go with your gut!

fiber blend

Is your digestive system weighing you down and making you feel sluggish? It's time to up the fiber!

1 cup almond milk

1 cup kale

½ cup blueberries

1 tbsp chia seeds

1 tbsp almond butter

¼ avocado, peeled

Add all ingredients to the blender and blend well. Add a little water if needed. Remember, the chia seeds expand, so the longer you wait to drink this, the thicker it gets.

✳ CHIA BOOSTER

Chia seeds have been used for centuries for endurance and sustenance. These tiny gray seeds are also known to lubricate dryness and are high in fiber, making them great for fighting and relieving constipation.

piña colada

Piña coladas are dreamy, creamy, and deliciously sweet. Here I've added something green and removed the rum, but you might not even notice.

½ cup canned coconut milk

1 cup chopped pineapple, peeled and cored

½ cup or 2 leaves kale

1-inch slice fresh ginger

Add all ingredients to the blender and blend well. If you don't have a high-speed blender, grind or finely chop the ginger before adding it to the blender. That way it will blend up more easily.

belly soother

Ate too much? This smoothie will help your body break down the food with healthy probiotics and enzymes.

1 cup papaya

1 cup romaine lettuce

1 cup coconut kefir, yogurt, or cultured coconut milk

Juice of ½ lime

1 tbsp raw honey

Add all ingredients to the blender and blend well.

*PAPAYA BOOSTER

Papaya contains an enzyme called papain, which is greatly beneficial for our digestion. It's helpful both if you've eaten too much or something heavy (such as a big steak), or if you're feeling bloated and having overall digestive discomfort, because it literally helps your body digest and break down food. Papaya is also believed to alleviate coughing and moisten the lungs.

blueberry lassi

Lassi is an Indian yogurt drink celebrated for its digestive and cooling benefits. It's perfect after a heavy, spicy meal as a light dessert, or even as breakfast! Here I swapped out the traditional cow's milk yogurt with coconut kefir. This is a perfect probiotic boost for those of us who don't tolerate dairy.

1 cup coconut kefir

½ cup frozen blueberries

1 cup spinach

1 tbsp raw honey

Add all ingredients to the blender and blend well.

pineapple
express juice

Pineapple and greens work so well together. The sweet, juicy pineapple makes up for any bitterness that the greens might add. Who knew something so delicious could also be so very good for you?

2 stalks celery

1 cup chopped pineapple, peeled and cored

4–5 leaves kale

½ lime, peeled

¼ cucumber

Put all ingredients through a juicer. Alternate between harder foods, like celery and cucumber, and kale and pineapple to help move everything through smoothly.

✳ PINEAPPLE
BOOSTER

Pineapples contains bromelain, a digestive enzyme that not only increases your body's ability to digest food well but is also believed to help destroy worms(!). Pineapple eases digestive discomfort, has anti-inflammatory properties, and is said to help remove "the summer heat," making it one very powerful fruit!

green juice light

I call this Green Juice Light—although it is a pretty hard-core green juice, the romaine and fennel give this drink such a smooth and delicious flavor, you'll forget all about the fact that you're actually drinking a healthy green juice! It's just that good.

¼ bulb fennel, with the stalk and green herbs

6 leaves romaine lettuce

½ lime, peeled

1 green apple, peeled and cored

Leaves of 1 stem mint

Put all ingredients through a juicer. Alternate between harder foods, like apple and fennel, and the romaine and herbs to help move everything through smoothly.

fine
fennel juice

The fennel gives this juice a refreshing and slightly licorice-y flavor that I absolutely love. (We Northern Europeans take licorice very seriously!) With both cucumber and pear, you end up with a super-smooth and delicious drink that is perfect even for the most skeptical of juice converts.

1 cucumber

1 pear

½ lime, peeled

⅓ bulb fennel, with stems and herbs

3 leaves romaine lettuce

Put all ingredients through a juicer. Alternate between harder foods, like pear and cucumber, and the romaine to help move everything through smoothly.

 **PEAR BOOSTER**

Pear contains water-soluble fibers such as pectin, which has been shown to help lower cholesterol and tone the intestines. In Chinese medicine, pear is considered a cooling fruit—perfect for people who tend to overheat, both physically and mentally.

INDEX

A

Açai, 48, 177
  Açai Green, 114
  Super Brazilian, 177
Agave, note about, 52
Apples, 93
  Apple Pie, 137
  Cool it Green Juice, 179
  Dandelion Bliss, 93
  Good Greens Juice, 161
  Green Juice Light, 193
  The Green Master, 91
  Green Monster Juice, 104
  Immunity Green Smoothie, 74
  Kale Energizer Juice, 180–81
Avocado(s), 42, 88
  The Bee-utiful, 152
  Greenest Green, 88
  The Green Kiss, 164
  Spinach, & Kiwi, 134

B

Banana(s)
  Chard, 142
  Copacabana, 111
  Go Go Goji, 168
  Matcha Shake, 175
  Seeds of Change, 112–13
  Spiritual Gangster, 174
Bee pollen, 46
  The Bee-utiful, 152
Beet It Juice, 103
Beets, 103
Berries. *See also specific berries*
  Northern Lights, 148
  Whey to Go!, 121
Blenders, 23–25
Blueberry(ies), 117
  Açai Green, 114
  Dandelion Detox, 92
  Fiber Blend, 184
  Hypnoparadise, 170
  Lassi, 189
  Power Breakfast, 117
  Purple & Green, 118

Brown rice protein, 40

C

Cacao, 48, 167
  Chocolate Mint Chip Shake, 167
  Dandelion Detox, 92
  Super Brazilian, 177
Carrots, 126
  Jessica Rabbit Juice, 126
Cayenne pepper, 91
Celery, 30
  All Greens Juice, 100
Cherries, 149
  Northern Lights, 148
  Red and Ready, 149
Chia seeds, 42, 44, 184
  Açai Green, 114
  Fiber Blend, 184
  Green Power Bliss, 84
  Seeds of Change, 112–13
  Super Brazilian, 177
Chocolate Mint Chip Shake, 167
Cilantro, 99
  Fiesta Juice, 99
  Jicama Slush, 98
  Mango Madness, 146
Cinnamon, 138
Coconut kefir
  Belly Soother, 188
  Blueberry Lassi, 189
Coconut meat
  Coconut Greens, 79
  Copacabana, 111
Coconut milk, 62
Coconut oil, 42
Coconut syrup, 52
Coconut water, 62, 174
Cucumber(s), 30
  All Greens Juice, 100
  Cooler Juice, 157
  Dandelion Bliss, 93
  Fine Fennel Juice, 194
  Good Greens Juice, 161
  Greenest Green, 88
  Skin Tonic Juice, 158
  Watermelon Medley Juice, 154

D

Dairy products, note about, 37
Dandelion Bliss, 93
Dandelion Detox, 92
Dandelion greens, 92
Dates, 52

F

Fats, healthy, 38, 42, 129
Fennel, 94
    Fall into Winter Greens, 94
    Green Juice Light, 193
    Juice, Fine, 194
    "V8" Garden Juice, 127
Fiber, 38, 44, 73
Flax seeds, 42, 44
    The Green Kiss, 164
    Seeds of Change, 112–13
Fruit juice, for smoothies, 67
Fruits. See also specific fruits
    organic, buying, 34–35
    seasonal, benefits of, 32–33

G

Ginger, 50, 87
Glass jars, 26
Goji berries, 50
    Go Go Goji, 168
Grapefruit
    Bittersweet Symphony, 77
    Green, 80
Green juices and smoothies
    blenders for, 23–25
    health benefits, 20, 23
    juice compared with smoothie, 20
    juicers for, 25–26
    measuring ingredients for, 71
    money-saving tips, 58
    nutritional benefits, 19–20, 23, 55, 64
    preparing juices, 27
    preparing smoothies, 24
    smoothie base liquids, 60–67
    storing, 58
    time-saving tips, 54, 57

Greens. See also specific greens
    fiber in, 44
    health benefits, 28, 30
    Mango Madness, 146
    raw, and thyroid issues, 33

H

Hemp protein and seeds, 40, 42
    Dandelion Detox, 92
    Seeds of Change, 112–13
Honey, raw, 52, 77

J

Jalapeños, 127
Jicama, 98
Jicama Cilantro Slush, 98
Juicers, types of, 25–26

K

Kale, 30, 133
    Apple Pie, 137
    The Bee-utiful, 152
    Beet It Juice, 103
    C Booster, 108
    Coconut Greens, 79
    Energizer Juice, 180–81
    Fall into Winter Greens, 94
    Fiber Blend, 184
    Go Go Goji, 168
    The Green Master, 91
    Hail to the Kale, 133
    Jessica Rabbit Juice, 126
    Morning Sun, 142
    Piña Colada, 187
    Pineapple Express Juice, 190
    Power Breakfast, 117
    Refresh Smoothie, 83
    Spiritual Gangster, 174
    Sweet Almond, 138
    Watermelon Medley Juice, 154
    Whey to Go!, 121
Kiwi, 134
    The Kiwi, 151
    Spinach, & Avocado, 134

L

Lemonade, Frozen Green, 145
Lemons, 145

M

Maca, 48
Mango(s), 146
    Madness, 146
    Morning Sun, 142
    Skin Tonic Juice, 158
    Sweet Almond Kale, 138
Maple syrup, 52
Matcha green tea, 67, 175
Matcha Shake, 175
Mint, 179
    Chip Shake, Chocolate, 167
    Cucumber Cooler Juice, 157
    Green Mojito, 141

N

Nut butters, 44
    Fiber Blend, 184
    PB & Jelly, 122
    Sweet Almond Kale, 138
Nut milk, 60–63
Nut milk bags, 26
Nuts, protein in, 40

O

Oats
    Power Breakfast, 117
Oranges, 108
    C Booster, 108
    Morning Sun, 142
    OJ and Greens, 87
    Peachy Green, 130

P

Papaya, 188
    Belly Soother, 188
Peaches, 130
Peachy Green, 130

Pea protein powder, 40
Pears, 84
    Fall into Winter Greens, 94
    Fine Fennel Juice, 194
    Green Power Bliss, 84
    The Green Kiss, 164
    Hail to the Kale, 133
Persimmon, 125
    Winter Wonder, 125
Pineapple, 190
    Cilantro Fiesta Juice, 99
    Express Juice, 190
    Good Greens Juice, 161
    Green, 79
    Green Goddess Smoothie, 97
    Green Mojito, 141
    Piña Colada, 187
Probiotics, 46, 183
    Immunity Green Smoothie, 74
Protein
    adding to drinks, 36, 73, 107
    types of, 40
Protein powder
    Açai Green, 114
    Green Power Bliss, 84
    Hail to the Kale, 133
    Hypnoparadise, 170
    PB & Jelly, 122
    Purple & Green, 118
    types to avoid, 41
Psyllium husk, 44
Purslane, 158
    Skin Tonic Juice, 158

R

Raspberries
    PB & Jelly, 122
Romaine lettuce, 30
    Belly Soother, 188
    Bittersweet Symphony, 77
    Cilantro Fiesta Juice, 99
    Cool it Green Juice, 179
    Frozen Green Lemonade, 145
    Good Greens Juice, 161
    Grapefruit Green, 80
    Greenest Green, 88

Green Goddess Smoothie, 97
Green Juice Light, 193
Green Monster Juice, 104
OJ and Greens, 87
Peachy Green, 130
Pineapple Green, 79
Refresh Smoothie, 83

S

Salad spinners, 26
Seeds. *See also specific seeds*
   protein in, 40
   Seeds of Change, 112–13
Spinach, 30
   Açai Green, 114
   All Greens Juice, 100
   Blueberry Lassi, 189
   Chocolate Mint Chip Shake, 167
   Copacabana, 111
   Frozen Green Lemonade, 145
   Green Mojito, 141
   Green Power Bliss, 84
   The Green Kiss, 164
   Kiwi, & Avocado, 134
   The Kiwi, 151
   Matcha Shake, 175
   Northern Lights, 148
   PB & Jelly, 122
   Purple & Green, 118
   Red and Ready, 149
   Refresh Smoothie, 83
   Seeds of Change, 112–13
   Super Brazilian, 177
   Winter Wonder, 125
Spirulina, 46, 170
   Hypnoparadise, 170
   Spiritual Gangster, 174
Stevia, 52
Strawberries
   Go Go Goji, 168
   Strawberry Fields, 173
Straws, 26
Superfoods, 39, 46–50
Sweeteners, 52
Swiss chard, 30
   Banana Chard, 142

T

Tangerines
   Banana Chard, 142
Tea, 67, 175
   Matcha Shake, 175
Thyroid issues, 33

V

Vegan protein blends, 40
Vegetables. *See also specific vegetables*
   organic, buying, 34–35
   seasonal, benefits of, 32–33
   "V8" Garden Juice, 127

W

Walnuts, 137
   Apple Pie, 137
Watermelon, 154
Watermelon Medley Juice, 154
Whey protein, 40
Whey to Go!, 121

Y

Yogurt
   Belly Soother, 188
   Northern Lights, 148

Acknowledgments

It takes tasters, shakers, movers, and makers to make an entire book loaded with smoothie and juice recipes. I would never have been able to complete this project without help and support from all these amazing people.

First of all, thank you to my beloved husband, Roald, my cheerleader, photographer extraordinaire, taste tester, and copy editor. Thank you for capturing beautiful images for this book. I would never have been able to do this without you, and your continuous love and faith in me. Thanks!

Also, thank you to my baby boy who grew inside me throughout this whole process— thriving and growing on all the greens I fed him over the months of recipe testing. Thank you for your patience and for allowing me to have all the energy I needed to complete this book before you arrived into the world.

I also want to thank my dear friends and family for all their encouragement, curiosity, and faith in me. Thank you for bearing with me throughout all my passionate health talk, green juice pushing, and smoothie tasting.

Thanks to Ann Treistman for bringing this whole concept to life and all the other fine people at Countryman Press for their outpouring of excitement, enthusiasm, and total belief in this book.

Thanks to the talented Patryce Bak for additional photography.

Last, but not least, thank you to all the juice bars and smoothie shacks that I've visited around the world. Thanks for all your inspiration and recipe ideas. Your dedication to healthy living is truly inspiring. Thanks for sharing your love for real food with the world.